ISBN: 9781658518192

First published: March 2020

Alexandra Paucescu

Just a Diplomatic Spouse

A true Story of Life

ക്ക‌ക

In loving memory of my grandparents

CONTENTS

CHAPTER 1- THE BEGINNING

I first thought about writing this book after I met a very dear and old friend of mine.

I was living in Berlin at the time and we had met after more than 20 years. We live on different continents and this was the first opportunity to meet after such a long time. We had been both exchange students in the USA while in high school and kept in touch now and then ever since.

We started talking about our lives, our families and he asked me how my life was. As he knew my husband was a diplomat, he told me he figured we had a pretty wonderful and relaxed life...'worry free', as he put it.

Indeed, if I start thinking about it, there are quite a lot of clichés when it comes to diplomats and their spouses. Most movies picture diplomats as perfect spies, always impeccably dressed and drinking cocktails every evening at exclusive parties, while their ever smiling wives are the epitome of elegance and grace. They are great housewives, polite hosts and raise perfect children.

I also remember how I used to look at the cars with the CD sign (diplomatic corps) on their license plates, when I was just a girl. Diplomats seemed so special. To me, living in Romania of the 80's, a communist country, where travelling abroad was forbidden for most of its citizens, visiting their countries of origin seemed like an unreachable dream. I always wanted to travel, go see the world, not just through pictures and movies. I also had my father's words in mind, which perfectly fit the minimalism approach of today: 'give experiences, not things'. He is and always has been a passionate traveller and always spent his money on trips abroad, on all corners of the world, instead of buying things that become useless after a short while. Memories last forever, travel opens your mind and heart...

Luckily for me, as for most of my countrymen, after 1989, when all the communist regimes in Europe collapsed one by one, we were finally free to travel wherever we desired.

Though diplomatic life was still a mystery to me, almost 20 years later, I entered into this fascinating world... Looking from outside, it is definitely a privileged life. You get to see the world, you meet lots of interesting and powerful people and have lifetime experiences. You live in a protected world that gives you immunity… only diplomatic, not for your soul and feelings though!

You've got to be strong to adapt, to get to know the rules of this kind of life and to make the best out of it. There is certainly more to it than just tax-free, nice housing, less parking tickets and special status, as most people from outside would think.

So, are you curious to know what's like to be the wife of a diplomat, to go from posting to posting, moving every couple of years? ...then this is a book for you! I wrote it to share my experience with you, my readers, and, meanwhile, maybe to help other spouses at the beginning of their own diplomatic journey, thriving with its difficulties that automatically come along. They all have to know that they are not alone in their struggle, their worries are common and that eventually you get used and enjoy your new life.

This way of living certainly has its share of stressful situations, times of deep loneliness, even despair, strangers that will come and go from your life. But it is also a life full of sweet memories, great experiences that will enrich your life and change you forever.

When you live in another country for years you discover it, as no city break or vacation will do, you really get to know the place and the people. You will live like the locals, you will start to understand them and eventually blend in. So this book is also like a small travel guide of the countries we lived in, through my own eyes, with my own local experiences... what I liked and what I hated the most, what I missed once I left the place and what I was happy to leave behind.

Every destination of my journey so far had its own flavour, its uniqueness and beauty, which I am happy to share with you now.

Moving is, as experts often say, the third most stressful situation in life, after the death of someone close and divorce. Besides the enormous amount of stress that comes with any new move, every step of my journey came with lessons I hope I've learned, knowledge and experiences which made me into what I am today. As a result, I see myself now a bit wiser, more patient and understanding, more organized and more open than I already was.

I entered this life when I was around 30. Funny thing is that while in university, a professor of mine kept telling me I could be good as a diplomat and that he would support me to it... I didn't listen as I was already working and I was pleased with my job and with my starting career in sales and marketing.

Some years passed by and I met my husband. He was already a diplomat and, as our relationship became more serious, I started wondering if I would really like to live the kind of life he was about to have, travelling abroad and living in different parts of the world for years, always changing places, houses, people... This was just about all I knew of this life... I guess this is almost the same as everybody does...

I talked to my uncle about it and he said I should not worry about leaving a house behind, a job, about moving to another country for a while... the only question I should seriously ask myself was if I was ready to leave all the people behind and go away with just one man, my husband, as he would be the only constant in my life for years to come (before we got the kids).I guess I should thank him now for his wise advice!

We eventually got married in New York, started our family life and got our first child rather quickly, while we were still living in our home country, Romania. I also got pregnant with the second one within the first 2 years of our marriage.

And then the first move came...

CHAPTER 2- VIENNA, AUSTRIA

While 7 month pregnant with my son, we moved for the first time, to Vienna.

As I think back now, it is quite remarkable I didn't feel too much pressure or concern about moving in a new city, in a new house and with no help around, except for my husband. Was he nervous about moving, about the novelty of his job abroad and all its implications and new responsibilities? Maybe... but he wouldn't say a word to me... I only remember his warm smile when he, to our great surprise, was waiting for us just before the baggage claim area in the Viennese airport (credit to his diplomatic ID). He had driven to Vienna few days ahead of us and he was greeting us to our new home town.

We were just a young family with one baby in our hands and another on the way, starting our new diplomatic life in Vienna.

Of course, it helped a bit that we already knew this beautiful city and we loved it. We have always enjoyed visiting the Austrian capital for a short city break or for a longer time. It has always been an elegant city with nice people and great atmosphere. Vienna has been declared for years in a row the best city in the world to live in, having the best quality of life and infrastructure for families with small children. And that is true, I can honestly say now!

We had some friends already living in Vienna and also some family of my husband's. So at least we had some guidance at the beginning, especially as I was going to give birth in a few weeks and needed a doctor, hospital... also a kindergarten for our 1 year old girl.

I usually do everything in a hurry, I am quick and organized (qualities that I surely got from my mother), and that really helped throughout our life of packing and unpacking. ☺ Within a week, the house looked decent and I was already in the park with our girl or discovering Vienna's beautiful city life. I was really starting a new life.

We had just moved from living in a quiet residential area outside the crowded city of Bucharest to the heart of Vienna. Our home was a spacious apartment, in an old building, an 'alt Bau' as they call it. It was just two minutes away from Rathaus (Vienna City Hall) and the Parliament building. I was walking everyday on the Ring (a circular boulevard around the old city centre) and in the so-called 'Inner Stadt', the core of the city, with its fancy shops and famous cafés. I was blending in with the busy locals, the elegant old ladies with their perfect styled hair and a string of pearls always around their necks, with crowds of enchanted tourists admiring Stephansdom (St. Stefan cathedral) and all the other beautiful buildings in the area. The impressive Hofburg Palace (Imperial Palace, now partly official residence to the Austrian President), all the old churches, the romantic Volksgarten with its ancient colourful roses, these are all testimony of a majestic imperial capital that hasn't lost any of its charm throughout the years. And I was living in the middle of it, seeing it every day. It was like a fairy tale.

I always thought I was a lucky person. I had my share of disappointments over the years, but generally life was good to me and the right people and events came into it as I needed them, at the perfect time.

So, to follow that, we found in almost no time a good bilingual (English and German) kindergarten for our girl. Everything was set and we couldn't believe our luck, as kindergarten places in Vienna are scarce for young age children and people register years in advance to make sure they have a place for their kids when the time comes. We did the same with our second child... we registered him the month he was born and actually started kindergarten one year later! Although usually difficult to get a place in a kindergarten, the city of Vienna is very helpful when it comes to families with kids. The city supports half of the price of any kindergarten (public or private), so basically anybody affords sending the kids to one, no matter how expensive it might be… also Austrian families with kids have all other kinds of social benefits, meant to encourage them to have more children and to raise the birth rates, quite low anywhere in Europe, for the last decades.

I was, as any young mother would be, concerned about my baby girl going to kindergarten. How would she manage, would it be hard for her not having me around for hours every day? … We never had any babysitting for our kids and we raised them by ourselves, no help from outside. This is quite unusual for Romanians, who are Latin people and, like Italians, are used to have the support and constant help and presence of parents, grandparents and other relatives in raising their children. But I always knew I would be a dedicated mother and I wanted to raise my kids my own way. The distance also played a very big role into this…

So, coming back to my daughter's first days in Vienna, I was worried about the transition… she had already changed the environment, leaving the house she knew, her room full of toys and our lovely garden behind. I remember the first few nights in the new apartment in Vienna were quite restless. She was not yet comfortable in her new room, crying every night and not going to sleep as easily as she used to.

Miraculously she loved the kindergarten from day one! The adaptation period, which is normal in any Viennese kindergarten, was very short and easy for us. They told us that we might get a clue about how easy it would be for her to fit in… they had this method: every morning, for the first few weeks, started with the same routine, so that the child would feel safe and start to recognize it as familiar. The first day, while I was sitting in a corner of the room, looking how she was discovering the other children and all the objects in the classroom, I was told that the less she came to me, the easier would be for her to fit in and start her little adventure away from me. And indeed it was! My girl was not a baby anymore. She loved the atmosphere, the other children's company and almost didn't want to leave. I was really amazed! She was for a little more than one year on this Planet, but had already learned the secrets of fitting in and how to make herself enjoyable to the others. I remember though, with such love, the look of joy in her eyes the moment she saw me, every afternoon, when I was picking her up.

She knew no German words, yet she managed just fine. And in a few months she already started saying words in German. The immense power of little children to adapt to new environment conditions never stops to amaze me!

The teachers from the kindergarten had told us not to worry… kids that hear more than one language from an early age start to talk a bit later, but in all the languages… and our girl heard three… so one can imagine the chaos and confusion of the beginning ☺ . Children also have the marvellous ability to switch automatically to the language they are spoken in and they will also reply in that language. Amazing!

The fact that the kindergarten was bilingual proved to be a wise choice for us. Beside the fact that, as diplomats, you can expect to travel the world, and English is a must for your children too, it was a very international environment. Lots of expats and also other diplomats had their children there, so our kids didn't feel any different from most of the children, talking in another language at home, at such early age.

When you move to another country, especially when you have children, medical insurance should be one of the main concerns. You never know when you might need a doctor and you definitely have to be informed about the medical system in the country of residence, how it works, where to go… As we are part of European Union, it was relatively easy for us, right from the beginning. As diplomats of an EU country, we automatically received standard medical insurance. This meant that we could have access to all medical services. In Austria most doctor appointments are covered by the basic insurance, but if you need a more specialized opinion or if you want to move fast you should go to a private practice. The best doctors usually have private practices most of the times. But no matter public or private, they are all very cooperative, nice and sympathetic. I will never forget all the help and support I got from the doctors and all the nurses while in hospital giving birth to my son. They would comfort me when I needed it, calmly explain all the procedures and assist me all the way, even though I was a foreigner, didn't speak any German and I was totally unfamiliar with the way things were supposed to be done. I cannot forget the day my son was born. I went relaxed to the hospital, to deliver a healthy baby boy, but I woke up few hours later in a completely different reality. He had neonatal pneumonia and had difficulties breathing on his own. Because he was only a few hours old, the condition was critical. He was taken to intensive care, all hooked up to machines, with big needles in his little hands, with monitoring sensors all over his tiny body. The view was heart-breaking, believe me! On top of that, I was not completely aware of his condition, at the beginning. I was recovering from C-section and had this sharp pain in my back, which initially made doctors fear it might be embolism, a very serious and potentially deadly illness. I can only try to imagine the pressure that my poor husband felt: in a few minutes his whole life had turned from bliss to total nightmare, with his son and wife in such a condition. Fortunately, God heard our prayers and we all got better. I recovered, my son responded well to treatment and, ten days later, we were able to happily take him home and put all this horrible experience behind us. I am forever grateful to all the medical staff who has helped us with such warmth and professionalism. While in hospital, we decided to keep all these details a secret. We saw no point in worrying everybody back home, from the distance. I was most afraid my Grandma would find out and might have health problems (due to her sensitive heart) because of the troubling news. Even more complicated was justifying the baby's absence to my aunt and uncle, who had come to the hospital in Vienna to visit us, and were probably wondering why they could not see him. I remember that I motivated it with his slightly premature birth (he had come three weeks earlier). They never told me if they really believed it. This terrible experience, deeply traumatizing for any new parent, made us both, my husband and I, more aware of how precious life is and how grateful you must be for each beautiful day you get to spend with your loved ones. Life can turn from wonderful to ugly in a second...

When moving abroad, you are alone, only with your family. You basically test your social skills from day one. You train your ability to relate to other people, to make new friends and to fit in. It can be very stressful sometimes and it proved to be impossible to many. No one trains you or prepares you for this! I've heard of other diplomats' families breaking apart and spouses going back home, or even worse, going to severe depression, because of it.

As a diplomat, you have your career that goes on, no matter which country you go to. Of course, you have new colleagues with each move, you learn new rules and respect the country's customs. But you are already in a group that you belong to, you have the sense of continuity that is very important.

As a spouse (most of the times a woman), like myself, on the other hand, you are alone. You decide to follow your husband and family but have nothing else to begin with.

You leave behind not only your house but your extended family, parents, siblings, all your friends that you made for years and also your job. You suddenly have nothing from all these and you have to start all over again, every time you move to a new posting, from zero. You lose entirely your independence, especially financially. You have nothing on your name... car, lease, even on the diplomatic ID, that you get when you start living abroad on a diplomatic mission, you will have your name and the explanation 'wife of...' underneath ...

This proved to be too much to many. And, I tell you, it is sometimes disturbing and hard to accept. At least at first it can be a shock, especially if you've led an independent life before!

Of course, you have the advantage and luxury of TIME... for yourself, for your family and for your children. Diplomats' wives don't usually work while in a foreign country, this is somehow accustomed and most of the times even clearly regulated. Most countries don't really encourage the diplomats' partners to work or have lucrative activities, there are a lot of boundaries and conditions that drastically limit your options, until you come to the conclusion that it's better to relax and forget about it...and eventually you realize it would be almost impossible to pursue a great career while moving every four to five years to another country, anyway…. So, except for the diplomatic functions you are frequently asked to attend, it's quite a lot of free time to live life and enjoy it.

But, if you were a busy person before the move, with a flourishing career, this might not be easy to deal with, nor enough.

You discover yourself once again, you are like a new born. You have to learn to live in a new world, everybody you meet is a stranger and you have to prove yourself everywhere as nobody really knows you and what you are capable of. What you have done before is not really of any relevance for the new life you are going to live.

To many you are 'just a diplomatic spouse', as I sadly remember somebody put it once, obviously being terribly disappointed when he discovered it was not the 'real diplomat' he was talking to... it sometimes can be demeaning and frustrating, as most of the diplomatic spouses are University graduates, cultivated women (or men)... but, as a 'diplomatic spouse', you are the 'plus one' on the invitations, seen more like an appendix to your husband...and it is only up to you to try to change that perception and become more, if possible!...

Diplomacy has its own ranking system, kind of similar to the military... so diplomats, the older and wiser they get, they advance into this hierarchy that comes also with more money, privileges, prestige and recognition.

You can see the little illustration I made about the general diplomatic hierarchy.

Of course, it may suffer small changes from country to country, but the main ranks are worldwide agreed and recognized.

DIPLOMATIC HIERARCHY

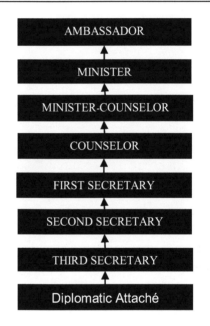

This hierarchy, as I learned for myself, applies also to the spouses. It makes a difference sometimes if you are the ambassador's wife or another diplomatic spouse of a lower rank diplomat. There are special events just for the ambassadors' wives and others, for everybody else. Depending on the diplomatic ranking of your husband, you are automatically placed in a category, a group of spouses and sadly, there are many who do not even bother to get to know you or look beyond that, to appreciate you for who you are as a separate individual. You are automatically appreciated more or less just because you're someone's wife.

As a spouse of a diplomat at the beginning of his career, as I was back then, I tried not to be affected by this automatic evaluation system and most of the times I succeeded. Sadly though, I have to admit that I have also met some arrogant wives of higher ranking diplomats at that time, much too preoccupied with their position, thinking they were far better and taking themselves too serious, looking down to anyone not on the 'same level' and refusing to even interact outside their circle... It can certainly be frustrating and it deeply hurts your feelings, especially if you are new into this world and don't understand what you've done wrong to deserve this kind of treatment. But I guess, in the end, this says all about them... even if they often don't realize it. I won't give any names but, if they ever read this book, they will recognize themselves for sure... I thought about it a while ago and I guess this kind of attitude comes mostly when they haven't lived in the diplomatic world for a long time, haven't started from the bottom and don't know how it feels on both sides. I believe it is also a lack of self-esteem, when you identify yourself too much with the position that your husband's job provides and you don't have anything else to say about yourself, as a separate individual. You demand respect from people without doing the same. The diplomatic world though is full of compassionate, educated and special people. I have met throughout the years remarkable women who taught me a lot, kindly guided me and shared the secrets of this life with me and, with their generosity, inspired me and others to do the same.

Over the years, as my husband quickly climbed the ladder of the diplomatic hierarchy, I've made friends from both sides and realized that most highly-educated people don't care too much about protocol and ranks, they know better to appreciate you for your own qualities and own conduct. I never forgot how I started and always tried to be kind, humble and grateful for my position.

As a diplomatic spouse it is, as I have already mentioned, up to you to become more, to prove your qualities and to use them, into the diplomatic circle and outside. You need to follow a certain type of conduct, be aware of the exposure and position you are in. Being someone with diplomatic status doesn't mean you don't have to obey the rules... on the contrary, I'd say you must be a moral example, always decent and elegant in behaviour, discreet but friendly. I remember, just as an example of how people have sometimes the wrong idea about the meaning of a diplomatic status that somebody asked me once: 'Oh, so you have diplomatic immunity... so basically you could kill someone and get away with it?'...

Being a woman with diplomatic status seems to be equally challenging when you are an active one, not just a spouse. I remember I was once invited to this panel discussion on the occasion of the International Women's Day (March 8th) at the United Nations headquarters in Vienna. The speakers were lady diplomats, Madame Ambassadors from different countries of the world. They all talked about the beauty of their job, sometimes the advantage to be the only woman in a room full of men in suits but also about the everyday struggle that they faced throughout their entire career, in order to keep a balance between the professional and personal life, or to have a fulfilled personal life at all. One was married to a freelance journalist, another to a trade specialist and other to a

21

diplomat. They all confessed that convincing their husbands to go travel the world with them was very difficult and in some cases it even resulted in divorce. Although we live in the 21st century there are still lots of prejudices about family dynamics and women's role in society. Nowadays still, although slowly changing, diplomacy seems to be a men's world as there are far less women diplomats and especially acting as ambassadors.

As for the diplomatic spouses, regardless of their training and academic level, most of them are 'housewives' or try to reinvent themselves professionally: doing free-lance work, becoming bloggers, influencers or doing volunteer work. Most of the times this professional reconversion may be difficult, tedious and not always successful.

When we moved to Vienna I wasn't speaking any German. I was fluent in English and French, beside my native Romanian, but that didn't help me much with my German... in fact it did not help at all... Vienna is pretty international and almost everywhere I could find somebody that understood and spoke English, so I was not really forced to learn German at all. Inside the diplomatic circles everybody spoke English at events but in time, I realized it was imperative to learn some German, at least to be able to understand my kids and my kids' friends when coming over.

I can think now of several funny moments related to my lack of German knowledge at the beginning… I will always remember my total confusion when meeting the nice old lady living just across the hall in our building. She always greeted me with a smile and the traditional (now I know this) Austrian 'Grüß Gott!' which sounded to me like 'piscot' meaning 'cookie' in Romanian☺. Oh, how I loved the sound of it, years later, when I was in Bavaria, Germany, on our ski holiday and our host greeted us with that!

Austrians are usually VERY polite. They would greet you, help you on the streets when you needed it, guide you nicely, but they can also be sometimes tough. It was not only once when I heard somebody giving me advice on how I should park better (like 10 cm closer or farther from the side walk…) and by the way, parking in Vienna can sometimes be difficult and very tricky… I was always stressed when parking, trying to understand all the signs hanging on the street poles, telling you where to park or not, on which days, hours… sometimes totally contradictory and really confusing, at least to me. This fear of parking in the wrong place got off I think from the day, only few weeks after our arrival in the city and after we had gotten our new diplomatic car plates. We used to park our car on the street in front of the house. My husband said to me quite relaxed that evening, looking outside the window: 'I don't see our car anymore… either someone stole it, or it was towed away…' Indeed it was… and so we found out where the car pound was, far outside the city…and how expensive was to park in the wrong place or at a wrong time…

But generally, the city centre was not very crowded, the traffic was ok and the parking places sometimes scarce, due to our central location, but enough.

The strict rules apply not only to cars, but to bicycles also. To our surprise we found it out quite early, as my husband was a frequent biker and he was stopped by policemen because speeding over the bike limit! Yes, don't smile… there is a speed limit also for biking on the special bike lanes in Vienna! ☺ And don't forget to use your helmet too, otherwise you might get a fine.

Living for years in this organized society made me appreciate even more the importance of rules and respecting them. These are the basic principles of the methods also used in kindergarten for kids. They are taught to be independent from a very early age but never bending the rules and never causing discomfort to the others around. I loved their educational methods and I can see the results years later in my own kids. Teachers were very organized and they taught the kids so, too. Everything had a very strict order and everybody respected it.

Austrians are good Catholics and, even if not all very religious, they have lots of church related public holidays. Which is not bad, except when you forgot to buy bread or milk and every single supermarket is closed. Closing time at stores is also quite early comparing to other countries and it seems nobody does any overtime in general, no matter where they work.

Sundays are for family only. There is no shopping on Sundays, except for the tiny emergency shops in the main train station, airport or at the famous hospital in Vienna, AKH... but these are well-kept 'secrets' that we found out later... I guess this is the same everywhere... somebody told us once that, when moving somewhere new, you buy most expensive for the first one-two years... as you don't know the place, the shops, the little secrets... that is true. The everyday secrets you will discover day by day.

We also discovered a lot of restaurants were closed for New Year's Eve. I come from a country where celebrating a new year is BIG. We go to parties, restaurants and celebrate all night long with fireworks and wearing our finest clothes. Austrians don't seem to share the same enthusiasm for the New Year, they celebrate it moderately in the public squares and streets (Graben is famous for that in Vienna) and then go to bed early, just after midnight. That was not a problem for us, though, as we had two small kids and barely got to see the midnight fireworks during the first years in Vienna. ☺

When the children got a little older, we discovered the lovely Wolfgang See, a beautiful mountain area near Salzburg, with small villages with painted fairy tale houses and lovely hotels, and we celebrated the New Year, for few years in a row, over there. We enjoyed the warm welcoming place, the hot wine (Glühwein) and the traditional cuisine. The live music bands also made the atmosphere very cheerful. And, at midnight, everybody would melt small pieces of lead and then throw them into a glass of cold water. Depending on the little figure formed out of the cooled metal, Austrians would know how the New Year would be. We amused ourselves and did the same, trying to interpret the meaning of the newly formed shapes of metal. It was fun!

Austrian food is usually very heavy. Pork is in almost every traditional meal, to the happiness of my husband☺.

The crispy delicious 'Schwein Stelze', the enormous spare ribs served with a beer on draft (best, on our opinion, in Prater amusement park, at Praterfee restaurant)... this is Heaven for any food lover who appreciates meat. Kids were also happy to have the tasty and famous Viennese 'Schnitzel' all the time. It is very thin but huge and often served with potato salad and cranberry sauce. Yammyyyyyyyy!

Of course, after years of living there, I also learned to prepare it, as well as the other famous traditional Austrian dishes: apple Strudel, cheese Strudel with vanilla sauce and Kaiserschmarm, my kids' favourite. Kaiserschmarm is a traditional dessert, originally coming from emperor Franz Joseph's time, a kind of thick pancake, cut into slices and served with apple mouse and sugar powder on top.

I was never very fond of the heavy cuisine, as I don't eat red meat, but I loved all those sweets and many more.

Vienna is famous around the world for its old, aristocratic cafés and cake shops. Wherever you go in the centre of the city you find one. Demel is the oldest (and finest, for my taste) in town, Oberlaa or Aida are also great, you can sit and have the best cakes in the world there! We used to go with our kids or our guests, enjoying the delicious pieces of culinary art, as well as the great architecture of most of these places. Oh, what a perfume of history they all had! The waiters though were not particularly friendly in all those traditional but very touristic places. But we didn't really care as the food was great!

When it comes to desserts, no successful Viennese kids' party was complete without the famous Sacher Torte, the traditional Austrian chocolate cake. It is apparently a simple recipe, chocolate cake and a bit of orange jam in the middle, but the kids simply adored it and wanted no other cake for their birthdays. You could find it all over the city, beginning with its original place of birth, the Sacher shop. It could also be easily carried around and away, as it was delivered in wood cases that protected it from damage. Very practical! It was however, a little too dry for my taste. I always preferred the 'Imperial Torte', made at the equally famous Imperial hotel on the Ring. Imperial cake is much creamier and remained my favourite until today.

Speaking of birthday cakes, we were surprised at first to learn that Austrians usually serve the birthday cake at the beginning of the party and the other treats later. It was completely the other way around from what we were used to back home, but we quickly adopted the new custom and did the same for our kids' birthday parties.

Austrians, and Viennese in particular, are very child friendly. They simply love kids. Almost every restaurant in Vienna has a special corner designed for children, special chairs, books to read or paper to draw on, special children's menus. Nobody minds if kids run, laugh or scream a bit louder... after all, they are just kids. I remember everybody smiled at me when pushing the stroller with my little baby and all were curious to see him, make fanny faces at him...I loved their open and friendly attitude.

They are very careful with kids and with others in general. There were also some funny moments related to this... once we were having a birthday party at our house for one of the kids. There were about a dozen of toddlers in our house, together with their parents... so I guess we were a bit loud... suddenly somebody rang the doorbell. It was not a late guest, it was the Police. My husband answered the door. After they excused themselves, they asked him politely: 'We were told there was a woman screaming from your apartment, is your wife at home? Could we please see her and talk to her?' Although they could clearly see what was going on, the officers insisted to see me, just to make sure I was in one piece☺. Of course, all was ok after that, but this funny moment always comes to our mind when we have parties at our home.

When I think about Vienna I also think about the best tap water I have ever tasted. I may sound a bit strange telling this to you, but it is important. Especially when you move away somewhere else where the quality of the water is not that good, you learn to make the difference. Vienna praises itself for having it delivered directly from the mountain springs, and anyone can sense it, indeed. It tastes delicious, low in nitrogen and with no traces of pesticides, it is always cold and safe even for small babies to drink! So, no need to buy still water, you have it already in your kitchen, at your disposal all the time, directly from the Alps.

And you also have it in any restaurant, free of charge, at any meal… and with every small cup of coffee. That is something I found interesting… all the lovely coffee shops serve delicious coffee, always with a small glass of water aside.

Viennese coffee is famous, they say this tradition goes back in time, from the first Turkish invasion. It is said that, once defeated, the Turks ran away but left the precious sacks of coffee behind, and this is how the Austrians made the first contact with it… truth or not, they make a good coffee nowadays! I am not a coffee drinker myself, but I will take my husband's word for that.

The quiet mornings at the terraces in the centre, with a coffee or tea in front, admiring the pigeons and overlooking the grand imperial buildings… these are memories that last for a life time.

Austrians love their morning time, and there were plenty to see, having something to eat or just a coffee, tea, a glass of Sekt or Mimosa (sparkling wine and orange juice) for breakfast. I admired that view every morning on my way back from the kindergarten, after leaving the kids there. Few weeks ago I was in Spain on holiday and I heard this song on the radio, singing about 'Alegria de vivir' (joy of life)… I guess I could also describe it this way… 'Alegria de vivir'… Austrian style.

All these beautiful moments of our Viennese life are stuck in my mind forever and I guess Vienna will always have a very special place in my heart.

It is the city where my son was born, where I started a new chapter in my life and I discovered so many new things and met so many people dear to me.

At first, meeting new people was tough. The first people you meet are the other diplomats and their families, but it is difficult and it can take a while to really make friends. For us, having children in kindergarten played a very big role into our social life. We were almost as happy as the kids when they received an invitation to a birthday party☺. At this young age people usually invited the whole family to party, so we got plans for the weekend, too. It was the start of some beautiful friendships. Of course, not all the time we found a good compatibility with other parents, enough to pursue the relationship further, but some people came close to our hearts and stayed there. We made friends with parents of our kids' kindergarten buddies, expats, foreigners or Austrians.

One of my dearest friends, Beatrix, was the mother of two lovely girls, colleagues of my children. I remember and miss now all the lunches we had together at our favourite restaurant, Ella's, in the middle of the old town, also our endless message conversations about anything: kids, life, clothes, shoes...

When moving abroad, even if you still keep in touch with your old friends from home (and I did that a lot), you still need someone near. And luckily I found her, this beautiful, elegant, stylish and cultivated woman, with similar interests and points of view. Our kids enjoyed each other and also our husbands were compatible, which is a very important aspect. So we started spending weekends, even Christmas Eves or Easter Sundays together and we felt very well with this warm and relaxed Austrian family. While I was abroad, I made a couple of friends but, as I found out later, most of these friendships didn't stand the test of time and distance... I guess they were not strong and deep enough... However, this one still stands. We kept in touch although we don't see each other often, they visited us in Romania and we visited them in Vienna, and, magically, every time, after the first few moments, we felt like we were never apart.

Vienna is not very far from Bucharest. One can reach it by plane in less than two hours or by car in approximately twelve hours. So we had a lot of people from home coming over to visit us. Whenever we had guests I had mixed feelings. First I was terribly thrilled to welcome them, but I was always exhausted for a week after they left. I had to clean, cook, drive them around, make city tours over and over again, and all that while I was also taking care of the two toddlers in the house. When our guests happened to also have small kids with them, you can imagine the total chaos around the house, and my nerves stretched to the max ☺

Our parents also came to visit us regularly. My only regret is that I couldn't bring my beloved grandma over to visit. Due to her old age, precarious health and heart condition, she could not travel by plane. She has always been the love of my life, my childhood hero, my living role model and the woman I adored with all my heart. So she was the one that I missed the most during our days in Vienna. Our long conversations on the phone and the little time I got to spend with her while we were vacationing in Romania could not heal the longing for her. And the hardest time was still to come. It happened in a nice winter day in January, when I got the call from back home that I wish I would have never ever gotten... in a blink of an eye she was gone... gone from this world, but never from my heart and memory. My Grandma, who had set the high standards of my social behaviour, who had taught me what was publicly appropriate or not, how to make polite conversation, always listen and think before talking, always respect myself and others, live life with joy, laugh and enjoy the moment, have lots of friends and keep them close, never go out with wet hair, never sleep without a blanket on or never cry in public... and so many more... The suffering was unbearable and, as I write this words now, more than 8 years later, I still have tears in my eyes. I can recall crystal clear our last phone conversation, the last time I saw her alive... but I also can recall thousands of beautiful memories and moments with her, her infinite love and loyalty to me and the huge admiration I had for this amazing woman, great human being, dedicated doctor, warm and dear friend to many. I read once that suffering never ends when you lose someone dear... you just learn to live with it. That's so true. I guess that, to everybody who had a beautiful childhood, and especially to the ones raised by grandparents, they are forever special. They represent the strong bond to a time of no worries, just pure love and innocence, which we all wish we would live again. But even if they are physically gone, grandmas and grandpas are forever in our minds and hearts, as love is forever. Until you have your own kids, you are not fully aware of the passage of time... once you have them and you see how fast they grow, you realize how fast time really goes by and never comes back.

In good or hard times, it is important to have friends close. Especially when you move away you should always keep in touch, keep that old connections and friendships alive. True friendship stands the test of time and distance. It is important for your state of mind and it will make you not feel lonely. I guess being posted on another continent is quite another thing. But in Vienna we felt good, our friends visited us quite often, we had our house full all the time and we loved it.

Austria is a beautiful country, with lots of high mountains, lots of glaciers you can ski on. You can also admire one of the highest summits in Europe, Grossglockner, 3798 m, with its forever snowy peak. Tirol is one of the main ski destinations for middle-class Romanians, so this also helped bringing people over, on their way to the slopes.

We are ski lovers ourselves and being in Austria meant going to ski regularly, though not as often as we would have wanted. Having babies or toddlers at home didn't help too much with that at the beginning. But as soon as the kids were eligible for ski school, we put them on skies. Kaprun, Zell am See, Hintertux or Mayrhofen were the places we chose for our ski holidays. Of course, if you are more into partying on the slopes, Kitzbuhel or Ischgl might be more attractive. But generally, the atmosphere is quite great on the Austrian slopes and in any ski resort. The after ski parties are full of joy and happy people dancing on popular old Austrian and German hits ('schlager') while enjoying a cup of hot wine, 'Glühwein', or some local beer. No matter where you go, you will find the same enthusiasm and mix of ski and fun. We enjoyed spending days in a row outside in the winter sun and fresh air, surrounded by snow and awesome scenery, with our children discovering the beauty of this winter sport from a very early age. And it payed off. They ski now faster and better than us and they love it as much as we do.

From this point of view we blended in perfectly. Austrians are in love with winter sports. They are very competitive and successful in all sport competitions related to it, they even have regular ski week trips in school. Almost everybody skis or does Nordic walking. Whether they ski in winter or they bike, jog or hike in summer, they like to move and enjoy nature.

They are a very sporty nation in general and this pleased especially my husband, a passionate marathon runner. The Vienna Marathon was an event celebrated by the whole city, usually in April each year, where thousands of athletes from all over the world gathered to run together through the old streets of the city. We were there every year, cheering and encouraging not only our own runner, but all the others. It was a very joyful event, a celebration of human endurance and love for sport.

Being such a devoted sportsman made my husband think later of competing in the Ironman competition. Ironman is basically a triathlon, but of extreme long distance. I cannot even imagine swimming 3.86 km, then biking for 180.25 km and running a marathon (42.20 km), all without a break. It made my head spin ☺ but after a year of hard and organized training, he did it. He would train almost daily, wake up at dawn and go bike outside in summer time or bike for hours on an indoor bike in our bedroom, until it smelt like something was burning… go swim regularly and run, run, run… It seemed like an ordeal to me but practice for a clear goal to him… When the time came we went to Klagenfurt, in the beautiful landscape of Carinthia, to be part of this incredible experience. We have seen all these men and women, coming from more than 60 countries and testing their body limits for a dream. It was impressive really! Imagine that, while my husband was competing in this race for a whole day, we went to the pool, we had lunch and dinner and, being tired after such a full day of holiday☺, we eventually went to the finish line and waited for him to end the race... I remember that I was particularly impressed by the wonderful atmosphere at the finish: all those people sitting on benches and cheering every time some new athlete was crossing the finish line, loud music on the background and the look of pure happiness mixed with exhaustion on the faces of all these sportsmen. Priceless!

As we stood in the stands, anxious to see our Ironman finish his race, I heard my little boy screaming with all his might, maybe to make sure he was heard in the uproar that was there: 'Mom, I have to go to the bathroom!!!' Imagine now how we came down almost running out of the stands (of course, when someone has two toddlers in hand, the meaning of this word is a little different). I was desperately looking for the toilet, I prayed it wasn't busy, and then we ran back as fast as we could (I literally carried both kids in my arms up the stairs). Needless to say, we got back seconds before my husband crossed the finish line. I don't even want to think about what it would have been like, that after three hours of waiting in the stands, we missed exactly the magic few seconds of the finish. Luckily, it didn't happen that way and, while Robbie Williams' song 'Let me entertain you' was loud in the speakers, our Ironman was fulfilling his dream.

It was a tough experience for my husband but he proved himself and to the others that, when you really want something, you can definitely achieve it. Chapeau!

Besides the interest in these extreme competitions, we shared Austrians' passion for staying outside, going on picnics and to the forests. But there is a generalized and perpetuated fear when it comes to sitting outside, on the grass, in the warm summer days. There are even jokes about it, they say the most feared animal in the Austrian forests is the tick. So most Austrian doctors recommend you get vaccinated in order to immunize yourself against Lyme disease, just to be sure and safe.

Whenever the weather allowed, we went on to discover the country's beautiful landscape. And it is really beautiful! You have lots to see in Austria! As a passionate amateur photographer, I took plenty of pictures throughout the years. Of course, nowadays there is not the same emotion as when I was little and I developed with my grandfather black and white films in the darkroom... I remember my childish impatience while expecting each picture to form and see if it was a good one or not. Now you can make a hundred pictures in a moment and choose the best one right away. But my passion for beautiful and inspired pictures remains and I could take full advantage of it during our trips. Even with our small children, we used to go away from Vienna quite regularly. It is difficult for me to name just a few of the amazing places we have seen over the five years we lived in Austria. Whether it is Hallstatt with its spectacular lake view and its salt mine, St. Wolfgang, St. Gilgen or other small town or village with beautiful traditional painted houses and red Geraniums flowers at the windows, or it's one of the many crystal clear lakes throughout the country, all the beautiful ski resorts we have travelled to, the cities of Salzburg, Linz or Graz... they all have their charm. We often enjoyed going to Neusiedler Lake, just an hour drive from Vienna, one of the largest lakes in Austria, on the Hungarian border. They called it the 'Viennese sea' as it is large, not very deep and very popular as a summer destination, with many summer resorts on the shores, beaches and boats sailing. Just lovely and very convenient for a short weekend getaway from the city in summer days.

Danube is also a big attraction. As this big river runs through the city, you can walk along the many canals, sit in a lounge chair, have a cold drink and admire the small boats sailing around. The 'Donauinsel' (Danube Island) is the most interesting though. It attracts lots of people in warm days. It is an artificially created island in the middle of the city, 21.1 km long but no more than 210 m wide. It is basically a vast recreational area full of restaurants, bars, night clubs and also a beach, 'Copa Cagrana', unofficially named after the more famous Brazilian one. Every summer, usually end of June, it hosts Europe's greatest open air festival, Donauinselfest, with more than three million visitors each year. Madonna gave her first Austrian concert here, in autumn 2008, in front of about 57,000 people. We were among them (back then we were just visiting Vienna and going to the concert). Donauinsel is also a paradise for sportsmen. My husband simply loved biking on the island. He used to ride there almost every morning in weekends, for an hour or two.

We loved going up on one of Vienna's hills, on Kahlenberg, covered with thick woods and winding roads, and with a really spectacular view from its top. On a clear sky day you could see not only the whole Vienna from up there, but also some farther away mountains.

Grinzing was another beautiful weekend destination to us. In fact, although a hill, part of the city, Grinzing is covered with vineyards and it is known for its good local wines that you can taste directly there, in the local 'Heurigen', small restaurants near the vineyards.

Not far from Vienna, in Lower Austria, we visited once Seegrotte, a former gypsum mine which, after an explosion that took place in 1912, was completely flooded and has thus formed a huge lake, which is today considered to be the largest underground lake in Europe. During the Second World War the Nazis used it as a perfect hiding place for a subterranean aircraft factory. Nowadays it is a touristic attraction and was also film set for 'The Three Musketeers' (1993).

Whenever we felt like hiking, we went to Hohe Wand nature Park, a beautiful rocky region 1000 m above sea level, not very far from Vienna, in Lower Austria. It is a very child-friendly area, with kids' trails in the forest, wild deer and small restaurants that serve traditional Austrian food.

In winter time, if you feel like skiing, in weekends you can drive to Semmering or Stuhleck, also not far from Vienna, and with mountains high enough for any taste.

Springs and especially autumns were reserved for going on a ride on the Danube valley, in Lower Austria. It is a beautiful region, full of vineyards and apricot orchards, along the Danube River. We particularly loved Durnstein, a medieval little town on the shores, with small narrow streets, pretty houses, an abbey and the ancient ruins of the Durnstein Castle, where, it is said, the English king Richard 'the Lionheart' was kept hostage upon returning from the Crusades. We went there many times, walking down the streets, trying all the local specialties (all kinds of apricot jams and schnapps) and enjoying the magnificent view of the whole valley.

Not far from there, one could easily reach also the Melk Benedictine Abbey, set on a massive rock, overlooking the Danube River and the Wachau Valley. It is a spectacular piece of art, a rich baroque style church with an equally impressive library, full of old manuscripts. 'The Name of the Rose', the famous novel written by Umberto Eco, also contributed to its fame.

Every trip in the region ended up with a stop for a special culinary treat called 'Steckerl Fisch'. It is apparently mackerel fish cooked on a stick at the fire, but with a special sauce on it. You can only find it there and IT IS DELICIOUS! No fancy restaurant, as you could have imagined, just some wooden benches along the river, fish and bread on a paper tray, but the taste is divine and like nothing else. We only found it again near Salzburg. It was something very similar, not mackerel but salmon, on the stick and with the same tasty sauce. But the original stays in Wachau, with its secret ingredients.

Years later, when we visited Vienna, we made a special trip to the area just to have that fish for lunch... and, of course, I had a piece of 'Imperial torte' later, in the city...

Also, in our Viennese days, I discovered Hugo, one of the most beloved summer drinks among locals, as well as the more famous Aperol Spritz. Hugo is a sweet cocktail drink with alcohol, made of sparkling wine, sparkling water, a bit of elderberry juice and few mint leaves. Of course, adding the right amount of these ingredients is essential. I am not a very big alcohol consumer, but Hugo became one of my favourite drinks when going out.

And when I say Hugo, the traditional yearly Summer Film Festival at Rathausplatz (City Hall Square) comes to my mind. It is there where I enjoyed the icy cocktail the most. This festival has a very simple but successful recipe: it brings good music and film together with good food from around the world. It is Europe's largest cultural and culinary festival. It projects famous operas and films on a huge screen in front of the City Hall (Rathaus), admission is free and you can enjoy the fine screenings while savouring some delicious food and cold drinks. Lovely atmosphere, just few minutes away from our home.

The same square was the place to be in wintertime, too. First, for the famous yearly Christmas Market, a mix of Christmas decorations, artisans' products and seasonal cuisine all under the many Christmas lights that surrounded the whole place and the park around it. I loved the huge lighted red hearts hanging from the old trees every year, the fairy tale atmosphere they created. It was kind of magic with cinnamon and vanilla flavour. And, of course, hot wine with spices was everywhere, served in fine big cups, nicely and differently decorated each winter season. I loved them, so I got a whole collection to remind me of all the hot wine and hot chocolate we drank there.

When the winter holiday season was over, a big skating rink was set in the same place every year, just to keep the magic of winter time longer, to the kids' happiness and joy. But Rathaus square has another special meaning to us... it is there where our kids learned to ride a bike, making tireless rounds around the park, delighted that they could finally do it without help. I can still remember this image: two happy small kids, their eyes full of pure joy, as only kids can have.

Although not usually my favourite season, I loved winter in Vienna. The city Christmas lights were magnificent all around the city centre. I could never forget the big chandeliers on Graben, reminding of the old times' grandeur, the big sparkling Swarovski crystals on Kärtner Street or all the small Christmas decorations in the shop windows.

It rarely snows in the city, so it was even more pleasant to go for a walk, admire its beauty in winter time, and have a bite of roasted chestnuts or potatoes. Be careful for the wind though! It is a very windy city, no matter which season. I realized very soon that the scarves, which almost all ladies (and even men) wore around their necks, were not only for fashion but for practical reasons too... so I also have now a pretty large collection. ☺

During our years in Vienna we tried to understand and live like the locals. It makes it easier for you and it is also nice to find out customs and traditions, sometimes very different from the ones in your country, but equally beautiful.

We bought 'Advent' Calendars with small hidden surprises for each day of Advent (24) before Christmas for our kids, we lighted up the four Advent Candles (each one for every Sunday before Christmas day), we looked for hidden eggs on Easter Sunday and even celebrated Easter twice (as we are Orthodox and traditionally 'our' Easter is one week later after the Catholic Easter Sunday). We loved celebrating, each year, Saint Martin's day, walking in the evening with the kids in the park and on the streets, with handmade little paper lanterns and singing traditional songs, along with the locals. And no real Saint Martin's ends up without cooking a goose for the whole family. So we did that too. We also decided to get into the atmosphere of Oktoberfest each autumn. We bought the traditional costumes (Trachten) and once also hosted a party related to that. My husband got a traditional pair of leather knee-length pants, a traditional shirt and also a hat from Tirol with its small feathers on a side. He looked very authentic. And I got my 'Dirndl' of course, the traditional Austrian and Bavarian dress, very flattering for any silhouette. You can find all these clothes in shops, especially around the time of Oktoberfest (which is in fact a German tradition from Bavaria) and, I tell you, they are not cheap. In fact they can get quite expensive, depending on the quality of the materials and the pattern they have (especially the women's costume).

One Austrian lady taught me that the Dirndl holds in fact a secret: depending on which side you wore your apron ribbon, you could signal if you were married or alone... left side for singles and right side for married women. So... right side for me it was ☺

One of the many lovely traditions that we gladly embraced while we lived in Vienna was attending the annual balls. There was a time of dancing and music that started with the Vienna Red Cross Ball at the City Hall and had its peak in January and February each year. The most famous was the legendary Opera Ball, held each year at the marvellous Vienna State Opera. It was where all the Austrian and some international celebrities were seen and was also live on TV.

But there are more than four hundred balls each year in Vienna, so you had where to choose from... These are usually special events for different people. There is a Flower Ball, a Doctors' Ball, a Lawyers' Ball, even a Coffee-house Owners' Ball or a Bonbon Ball. They all had the lovely waltz music of Johann Strauss and other talented composers in common! I loved that time of year. I loved the long elegant dresses and long gloves I got to wear, all the lovely people all dressed up. I especially admired the first dance of the debutants (young ladies always wearing long white dresses) from the Waltz dance schools, and even if we were not the best waltz dancers in the world, we had a great time each year. Listening to good music with a glass of Schlumberger Sekt or even 'Österreich Gold' (Austrian sparkling wine with small 24K gold pieces inside) in your hand, this would enchant anybody! These lovely events take you back in time hundreds of years, and even if you hear also modern disco music, the feeling is the same.

When it comes to music, Vienna is the 'queen'. The famous Opera house, one of the most prestigious in the whole world, stages each year hundreds of performances. All the great sopranos and tenors in the world proudly come to sing there. And, although tickets are completely sold out months in advance, we managed to attend a few shows, including my favourite, 'Madama Butterfly' by Giacomo Puccini. Years later, I took the kids to see it too, but in another city.

Vienna is also a big name on the map of modern music. Most of the European Tours of the greatest singers these days included the city. So we got the chance to see lots of artists live on stage, some just minutes away from our home.

My life was pretty full those days. I had my daily routine, the usual life of a mother with two small kids, a house to take care of and also diplomatic functions to attend, so it was pretty annoying when there were people asking me what I was doing all day… by the way, this is one of the worst questions you can ask a 'stay-home mom'! ☺… There is never a dull moment, trust me! I was my family's nanny, cook, personal driver, secretary, hair stylist, fashion consultant, personal shopper, finance director, travel manager, event coordinator and entertainer or emergency nurse.

But eventually, at some point, after both kids started kindergarten, I felt it was not enough. Life was settled and I felt that I needed something else beyond my home and family routine. These kind of feelings I guess are normal at some point and happen to most of stay-home mothers. But I had turned into one overnight, once we started moving from Romania, and the first years didn't let me think about it too much, as I was pretty busy. After your kids get a little 'older' though, you start thinking again about your role into society, you feel you can do more than just dusting the house and raising kids. You remember your life before the kids, sometimes with much action and deadlines, adrenaline and the satisfaction of things well done. You realize that, as much as you love your new life, you still miss at least parts of all those times and you don't want to be just 'a lady who lunches', as they call it.

So I started looking for other activities I could do in my hours of free time away from the children. I started learning a bit of German, also took Italian classes. Italian is a language I had always wanted to learn, as it is quite similar to Romanian and not very difficult for us to learn. I had this small group of people at the Italian Cultural Institute that I was meeting every week for the class. I enjoyed the relaxed and friendly atmosphere but there was not too much action there, too.

One day, a friend of mine told me about this foundation, United Nations Women's Guild. Maybe you don't know but there are four United Nations headquarters around the world. The main one is in New York (USA), there is another in Geneva (Switzerland), one in Nairobi (Kenya) and one in Vienna. The United Nations in Vienna (UNOV) has office, since 1980, in the Vienna International Centre (VIC), a modern building complex near the Danube, home to also other few international agencies. This foundation was located in the same building with the United Nations. My friend suggested that I should reach out to them, maybe I was interested to join. So I did… and with that, a whole new chapter in my 'professional' life opened, with infinite satisfaction and meaning. I have always been a compassionate person but I had not had the chance to do some change for the better in someone's life other than my immediate family and friends… and for the first time I had the chance to do that.

I remember, like it was yesterday, the first meeting I had with the ladies from the Guild in the UN cafeteria. They greeted me with such warmth and welcomed me to their group. I discovered, within the walls of the UN buildings, these ladies, mostly wives of UN staff but also some diplomatic spouses like myself. They are doing a great job, raising money for different causes throughout the world. I saw then what compassion, kindness and determination could do to make a change in someone's life.

These ladies voluntarily put in many hours of work into different projects and events, in order to raise as much money as possible and try to do some good somewhere in the world, where they are asked to help. UNWG is funding projects that help children and mothers all around the world. It originally started at the UN headquarters in New York with just some home baked cookies on a small table, many years ago. Since then, charity luncheons, language courses, yoga, dance classes, seminars or the already famous International Festival Bazaar are only a small part of the activity of the Guild in Vienna. I was welcomed and I started participating in the events, sharing my former experience in sales and marketing and getting involved in as many activities as I possibly could. I had the satisfaction of a job well done, I participated actively in raising the money and also took part in the process of choosing the projects to be funded. I read projects and studied them, saw the different, sometimes desperate situations that needed our help and I was deeply impressed by many. You cannot imagine how little sometimes is needed, to save some lives or make some people happy and safe... Some people would ask for help to build up a toilet in their school, to repair a roof, paint some walls in a classroom or to simply buy a cow to have something to eat... It is really sad we still have this in the 21st century... you realize once more that your problems are nothing compared to this... or, better yet, you do not have any real problems at all!

Becoming aware of this terrible world reality only determined me to do more, get more involved and have better results. I helped organizing the International Festival Bazaar, a lovely yearly international event with traditional products and food from more than 80 countries. People from all over the world would donate handcrafted products or cook food from their own countries for helping the Guild in raising money. This event has lots of visitors and it is a real success each year. It has indeed become a Viennese tradition before the Christmas season. Of course, organizing this big event proved to be more complicated than I had thought before starting, a lot of logistic to take care of and to synchronize, cut down costs as much as possible (luckily more experienced members were always there, involved in all processes)... but there were also other more delicate parts of planning...we always had to be careful how we arranged all the stalls, as there were countries that didn't like to be seated next to each other, due to political or historical animosities, so once again the diplomatic skills in all of us had to be put to work.

By being part of all that I learned a lot, from interacting with different people from all nationalities to analysing funding projects, making decisions related to fundraising and organizing charity events. All with the immense help from some of the members, extremely wise and kind ladies.

Sandya from Sri Lanka, Kalpana from India, Cathy from Canada, Gill from UK, Patricia from Argentine, Nadia from Morocco, Louise from Cameroon … thank you all, I am forever grateful for the way you took me under your wing and helped me grow!

I remember something I heard in one of our events, something that pretty much sums up the meaning of all the work at this beautiful foundation. It was this quote by Forest E. Witcraft, saying '100 years from now it will not matter what my bank account was, the sort of house I lived in, or the kind of car I drove…but the world may be different because I was important in the life of a child'… no other words needed… if you can help, just do it.

Our meetings, the plans we made for new events, all the preparation and the adrenaline of organizing events offered me the missing piece from my life at the time. It also offered the support group that we all need in life, especially when we live abroad. It came with the chance to meet new and fascinating people, make new friends and learn from their experience of the diplomatic world or life in general. I felt good about my life and I had a meaning!

Diplomatic missions are different from country to country. It depends from which continent you are, what kind of political regime is back home, how rich the country is and so many other factors. So, although all diplomats, there can be great differences in terms of life style, actions and conduct. And when you are living into this community, you realize it pretty soon. Some travel the world with nannies and cook after them, others just by themselves. Some with lots of luggage, others with just few suitcases.

Although not superficial, this world is also governed by appearances. It matters how you look, how well you dress, what kind of clothes you wear. For men it is always a suit and for women the elegant style is required most often. Depending on the time of the events, there is a certain strict dress code, not too flashy, always smart and feminine (for ladies), that is mostly appreciated. It was not very difficult to me to fit in, as I have always liked feminine dresses and high-heel shoes. So it was always a pleasure to go to events, all dressed up and surrounded by people with similar appearance.

I had my doubts at the beginning, as I am sure any diplomatic spouse had... Will I be up to it? Am I wearing the right clothes for a certain event? Am I behaving the way I should, am I saying the proper words?... But with time comes also the confidence. Over the years I also learned the main dress codes and their meaning. Some of it you usually know from your 'previous life', some you learn from the others around you and, in time, you get really confident with your choices. But it is always better to check and ask before, than feeling awkward later, if you find yourself completely inappropriately dressed for a specific occasion.

'White Tie' is the most formal. It usually requires elegant tail jackets and white ties for men and long evening gowns with above-elbow gloves for women. It is usually recommended when attending balls, opera representations and most formal dinners. Part of this is also sometimes required in some countries when being formally accredited to the president or monarch. Long time ago, in the 1800, there were special gala uniforms worn by diplomats at special ceremonies. However, they were mostly abandoned by the 20th century.

'Black Tie' means wearing tuxedo or smoking jacket, usually a bow tie for men and also floor-length dresses for women.

Dinner jacket means a dark-coloured jacket or dark suit for men. Always wear these with dark polished shoes and dark socks, long enough not to see the bare legs while seated!

'Cocktail' means a bit more relaxed but still very elegant style. It is normally associated with dark suits and silk ties for men and knee-length elegant dresses with high heels (preferable) for women. Remember: NO boots are allowed, no matter the season or weather conditions!

'Casual' does not mean 'jeans and sneakers', as one might think...nor very short dresses, shorts or short-sleeve shirts for men. When being invited to a breakfast, lunch, daytime function, garden party or tea-time meeting, you should wear a light grey or beige suit (especially on summer days) for men and daytime but still elegant dresses for women. Depending on the type of event, sometimes hats and gloves may be required (usually specified on the invitation).

Some events require wearing your country's national costume, and it is such a nice scenery to see the diversity and beauty in these, when gathered!

I confess I had never had a national costume before going on our first mission, but I have more than one now and wore them proudly on the appropriate occasions.

However, when not sure about what to wear or not very clearly specified in the invitation, my advice is to better ask while confirming the attendance!

Vienna is a city with lots of shops and boutiques, people love to dress up and so you have a rich shopping offer. If you think you do not have the right dress to wear, go buy a new one… there are plenty to choose from. I confess I am a fashion lover and I, like most women, love clothes, shoes, bags… So I started exploring the city, discovering the best fashion boutiques, latest trends, nicest local producers and shop owners. The list is veeeeery long ☺ It always starts with the famous shopping street Mariahilfer Strasse, but if you ever go to Vienna, you should also not miss 'New one by Schullin', a pretty Austrian jewellery shop near the famous city cathedral Stephansdom. I loved their fashionable silver or golden jewellery, not very expensive but easy to wear. When it comes to jewellery I have to mention Frey Wille, too. It is a well- known Austrian enamel jewel manufactory, with colourful vivid designs. Costly but eye-catching…Right around the corner from the city Cathedral you should stop by the famous shoe house 'Denkstein', with its most fashionable and most beautiful shoes in town. If you feel hungry go next door to the Manner Waffles store and get some famous pink packages filled with the delicious traditional Austrian sweets. You will find all the great names of the fashion industry in the 'Goldenes Quartier' (meaning the 'Golden Quarter'), right in the heart of Vienna, with their polished windows inviting you to step in. I am especially proud of Musette, a 100% Romanian shoe brand that opened its flagship store in the core of the city, while I was living there. If you are thinking about winter and planning to head to the slopes, a visit to the Sportalm store, Kitzbühel's original ski and winter fashion clothing company, should be good. Although quite flashy and sometimes unconventional, their costumes are of an exceptional quality and bold design. If you like the more classical look, Herman Maier, the famous Austrian ski champion, waits for you with his winter collections in stores. Of course, I cannot forget about Parndorf, a large outlet mall with a variety of brands, which is only 40 minutes away from the city. You will find that the offer and the prices there are unbeatable, worth the ride. If you have time and flair for good shopping you should also stop and check the small vintage stores that are basically everywhere, especially in the centre. You will be surprised to discover the best of brands on their shelves, clothes and shoes, most of them in perfectly good condition or even brand new. I tell you, Vienna is great for shopping!

Vienna has been unfortunately, especially in the last 10 to 15 years, also a medical destination for Romanians. Its famous AKH hospital, one of the largest in Europe, has treated thousands of Romanian patients and it is well known for its highly qualified doctors and revolutionary treatments. While in Vienna I managed to help some people from back home getting treated there. Although quite expensive, the services were great.

When you live the diplomatic life, time really flies. You have so many events coming and going that you don't even realize when years pass by. The duration of a diplomatic mission varies from country to country. For most of us it is three to five years. Asian missions are usually shorter (three years) but most of the time the Asian diplomats are required to do two or three missions in a row, before returning home for a break. Some countries have this rule which requires that their diplomats do a posting on each continent. Others are more relaxed and can choose their destination (of course, from the ones available at the time). But everybody lives more or less the same kind of life, not knowing where they are going to be in a few years, in which country, on which continent. Long term plans are a joke… and this can certainly be frustrating and intimidating for most people who do not have to worry about it.

So the day that we had to leave Vienna eventually came... Packing was not difficult but it took a lot more time than at our first move, five years earlier. We had at least twice as much stuff to move away, lots of voluminous toys, clothes, pieces of furniture, books and many more. When moving you just realize how much you buy and store in a house... although we knew our stay in Vienna would be temporary, we always found some beautiful carpet, a leather chair or a nice decoration which begged to be bought.☺ The house was full and now needed to be emptied. I remember that we decided we were going to store all boxes in a room until the moving day, and, in the end, the room was completely filled. Although I had bought tens of boxes and tape, they never seemed to be enough. So I decided to look for used boxes, instead of buying more new ones. I went to the supermarkets around the corner and asked the people there to save all the big boxes for me. Otherwise they would have thrown them away, I guess... So, almost every day you could see me on the boulevard carrying big empty boxes... and soon the 'luggage room' was full of banana boxes from Africa or others used to carry fruits or cans from South or North

America… we are living in a globalized world after all, aren't we?

The truck was one day loaded… I still have this vivid picture in my mind, of my two small kids caring their own toys down the stairs, helping the people from the moving company to load 'our life' into the big truck and be on their way . My children had broad smiles on their little faces while we had the anxiety of the adults who must change their life completely, once again... I can honestly say, last day in Vienna was one of the most difficult days of my life, until now! The morning when I left the house that had been our home for five years, I felt like I also left a small part of my heart behind. Seeing those empty rooms and corridors, once full of kids' laughter, where I had once seen them run, try their first steps... it was overwhelming and sad!

Vienna was extremely good to us. One child born there, lots of fun memories, important achievements, things we've learned, dear people that we have met and bonded with… we are forever emotionally attached to this beautiful city. We have lived a lot in five years!

But… as it is with every diplomatic mission, it was time to end it and open a new chapter in our lives…

Karlskirche, Vienna

Seegrotte, Lower Austria

Steckerlfisch- the most delicious local fish

Vienna's famous debutantes' waltz

Durnstein, overlooking the Danube

UNWG Christmas Charity Bazaar

Ironman Klagenfurt finish line

Hohe Wand, Austria

Schönbrunn Palace, Vienna

Charity Lunch

Christmas market in front of Rathaus

Winter time in Vienna

Madame Tussauds Museum, Vienna

CHAPTER 3- BERLIN, GERMANY

After a year spent home in Romania, we started another diplomatic mission in Germany's capital, Berlin. As we had discovered a year before, after all, there is life after moving ☺ ... so it was time to move again.

For me it was a completely new destination. I had never been to Berlin before and I have to admit I was a bit anxious, but I didn't have too much time to think about it, as we found out our new diplomatic destination only one month in advance. The children were thrilled though and that was most important to us. I had heard from other colleague diplomatic spouses that moving was easy at the beginning but it had gotten harder with kids reaching adolescence, when they usually make more solid friendships, they feel stronger about people they bond with, maybe they fall in love for the first time and they do not want to move away anymore. I even heard stories of diplomats forced to leave their kids behind, in boarding school, so they don't move around so often... I cannot imagine such a thing for us, as I am deeply attached to my children and wish to spend as much time as possible having them around. Luckily for us, those times of hard decisions had not come yet, so we were all looking forward to our next adventure, our new life in Germany.

Of course, the fact that we had previously been posted to Vienna, was an important asset and helped everybody. We managed to fit relatively easy although Vienna and Berlin are very different. The children spoke German fluently and so the transition was even smoother than it had been returning home, a year ago. This should not come as a surprise, as they spent most, if not their entire life, abroad.

The German language that Austrians speak may defer a bit from the German spoken in Berlin and in Germany, in general. We figured this out rather quickly. The children were a bit surprised at the beginning about the different accent they heard but they switched to the new one in an instant, with no effort nor remorse. Even with my poor German knowledge back then, I could figure it out that there were some differences. One can easily hear the difference between Germans and Austrians talking, and we felt this even stronger, some years later, when returning to Vienna for a visit.

We were in Germany now and we had to switch from our 'Viennese German'. So we started calling the potatoes 'Kartoffel' instead of

'Erdapfel', the tomatoes 'Tomaten' and not 'Paradeiser', the apricots 'Aprikosen' not 'Marillen', even the traditional question at any supermarket: 'Do you need a bag?' changed from 'Sackerl?' in Vienna to 'Tüte?' in Berlin. Small differences that made us laugh sometimes, at the beginning of our Berliner adventure. It proved more difficult for me though to try to make people understand and get them to help me find my favourite autumn treat, grape must, in stores, the first fall. I was looking for 'Trauben Most' everywhere, as they called it in Vienna...I even tried to explain the fabrication process to some, in order to help me find it ☺ … no luck... all I got, to my disappointment, was a simple grape juice...until one day my husband accidently saw the delicious drink on a shelf in store... Hurrayyyyyyyyy! It was the beloved 'Federweiss', white or red... always a pleasure to taste!

Of course, besides these details, there is the complexity of this language that discourages a lot of people when starting to learn it. I decided to study it more seriously while in Berlin and I can say now that I talk, listen and understand it, but I still think hard before choosing one of the famous articles 'der, die, das' (probably most of the time I still choose the wrong one ☺) or struggle to remember which is the right word for something. It is understandable, I guess, when, for example, the same verb, 'suchen', means 'to look for', 'to visit' (be-suchen) or 'to try' (ver-suchen), just by adding a different preposition in front. And this is just a tiny example. No need to add that the structure of a sentence in German is completely different than in most languages I speak and that you usually read a whole sentence just to find the verb at the very end... or that all nouns are written with capital letters, maybe they consider them more important ?!... I read that someone said once that life is too short to learn German... indeed, maybe it is ☺

Moving has never been easy to anybody, in general. When you see your new house full of unpacked boxes, filled with lots of things that need to be organized and put into place, you might feel a bit discouraged, at least for the first few moments... for me it was not the first time anymore. But moving so often has also its advantages... you get to redecorate your home every four, five years☺. You have a new house, new furniture... just let your mind free and the inspiration flow. As my passion for interior design grew constantly, I learned to search and find the best offers for furniture, rugs, curtains, lights, to use the available space more efficient, match everything together as well as to make the house as comfortable and inviting as possible. Although a bit overwhelmed at the beginning, I got to work and finished in record time, just three days after our flight to Berlin. I had the help of all my family, the kids arranged most of their clothes and toys in their room. My husband did his part too, he went out and bought, in record time, whatever I needed in the house, from more hangers to small cupboards and even a washing machine. My back hurt for a week after this 'marathon', but at least the house looked decent and functional and everything was put pretty much into place. It was madness though... we visited the furniture stores almost daily for the first week, in order to get all the stuff we needed☺. I can honestly say I know now every corner of these stores by heart ☺

After we settled in, the school search began. Moving to another country is always stressful, but moving with school-age children is at least twice as much! Every age comes with its problems, I guess... When you have small kids, you are looking for the perfect kindergarten. But the real headaches begin later. Choosing the right school is never an easy task. There are so many things to consider and you are never sure you have made the right choice. You try to do a thorough research, consider all options, think about the well-being of the children, compare different schools, read forums and reviews and try to project the possible future, although it is almost impossible. I guess every responsible parent knows that, nowadays a good education, even from an early age, is the top asset and the best present that you can offer to your children, for a good comfortable future.

Unfortunately, we didn't have much time to choose a school, as the new school year was about to start in only two weeks after our arrival in Berlin. While we had no problem with finding the house to live in, choosing the right school proved to be quite tricky. Our children spoke German fluently, so we decided there was no need to send them to an international school for now. I guess that, as a diplomat, you will always have that as a first option, especially in countries where children do not speak the language they will be taught in or there are security or educational issues. But Germany praises on its top education and we saw no reason to choose something else, especially with our children speaking German so well. We also wish our kids to be raised in the real world, with contact to the real German life, not too pampered nor spoiled, and in a varied environment, outside the diplomatic circle. So we looked for a good German school as close to our house as possible. Our first option, an evangelic school, proved to be fully booked and, although we are theoretically on their waiting list, for the last four years we haven't got any signs for available places... We found few other options and eventually decided for the closest to our home. It seemed a nice school, newly renovated. The Principal welcomed us warmly, so we were pleased at the beginning but later decided to move away.

We were new in town and completely unaware of the big differences between different parts of this huge city, with more than 3.5 million people, many nationalities and backgrounds.

Our home was in the centre district, called Mitte, just a street away from where the famous Berliner Wall used to be. No wonder that, when I tried to find our building on Google maps, days before our arrival, all I had seen were just trees and bushes... the building was brand new, built on the former east- side of the Wall, just on the observation zone. Even some postmen had troubles finding the address, at the beginning.

Although surrounded by new and modern buildings, just a short walk from the beautiful Gendarmenmarkt Square or famous Brandenburg Gate, the building was also close to a more exotic neighbourhood. I remember that one day we were lost on our way home and we got to drive to this street were almost all stores had Arabic and Turkish names, it was like we were all of a sudden thousands miles away, in another country. I had not seen such a big discrepancy in scenery in my life. It was in Neukölln, the district with the largest migrant population in Berlin. Even closer to us was Kreuzberg, with its traditionally big Turkish community, dating back to the 50's, when they had all migrated to Berlin, in order to help with the city reconstruction and later decided to settle permanently. Although living in Berlin for more than half a century, part of this large community doesn't seem to be fully integrated into the German society.

Sometimes later, we learned that this part of town may be more dangerous at night than other Berliner districts but it is also full of nice restaurants, with delicious food from all corners of the world. Oranienstrasse is one of the famous streets there, full of traditional restaurants, bars and with a vivid night life. It was also one of the first places everybody asked me about, when coming to visit us in Berlin. It is usually mentioned in any tourist guide about the city and regarded as very youngish and trendy. It looks a bit shabby and might not give you a good impression at daytime, but, once the night lights turn on, it is a completely different thing. It has a special vibe and young atmosphere. You can smell freedom all over, mixed with strong flavours that invite you to taste all kinds of food.

But for us, coming from the neat, dust-free, traditional Vienna, the change was quite drastic at the beginning. I made a mistake that I've learned not to make ever again. I was constantly comparing our Berliner life with the one we had in Vienna... the streets, the buildings, the people... everything seemed sooooooo different... and not exactly to my taste, at least at the beginning.

Berlin is the largest city in Germany (3.7 million people) and only the second most populous city in Europe, after London. It has the diversity of any big metropole in the world. You can find anything in Berlin and you can live any kind of life you wish: hippie, bourgeois, aristocratic... you name it... It is also a city that has been through a lot. It had its share of flourishing years but, during WW II was heavily bombed and almost completely destroyed. I once saw this map, at the History Museum in Berlin. It was very graphic. It showed the city before the war and immediately after it. Almost nothing remained in place. A tragedy. So the city is now a very interesting and unique mix of remains of the old buildings, some of them identically restructured, post war buildings and more modern ones. The way they succeeded in rebuilding a city, once in ruins, is remarkable. They are still doing it today. Actually, as I am writing this book, there is a big construction site very close to our house. They are rebuilding the Imperial Winter Palace, across the Berliner Dome (another grand edifice destroyed during the war and repaired in the 60's). The palace will have the old day's appearance but a modern functionality. It is built on the original site, following the demolition of a former tern huge building that had been built instead by the East German regime. The splendour and elegance of this part of the city will finally be restored.

Berlin has a unique history, it is a city that has been tragically and brutally divided after WW II. The famous Berliner Wall lasted from 1961 until 1989. It separated the city in two. The Western part belonged to the democratic part of the country (Federal Republic of Germany) and the East to DDR (German Democratic Republic), under the communist regime, with its strong Soviet sphere of influence, as all other central and eastern European countries (including Romania). So the soviet architecture is also present even nowadays, in the eastern part of the city, with its austere and soulless appearance. When you travel from east to west in the city, it is impossible not to see the big discrepancy between all these enormous apartment buildings in the east and the lovely neighbourhoods with impressive houses and lots of lakes and woods, in the west. All these make Berlin very special and also different from any other city I have visited before. I can only try to imagine the shock of a visitor in the 90's, after the fall of the Wall, as I figure the differences were far greater than they are today.

The fact that this city had a very special and tragic history, you can figure out quite soon. Everywhere you walk around Hackescher Markt area, you can find small shiny metal plates on the ground, with names of Jewish people, who used to live in that area and who were deported and then killed by the Nazi regime. They are everywhere. In fact, one of the former concentration camps lies not far from Berlin, in Sachsenhausen, and can be visited. Terrible scenery and a living proof of the horrors of war. There are buildings in Berlin (I found a church on Sophien Street) that still have holes in the external walls, living proof of the battles during those times. From time to time I used to hear on the radio that a street or area in town was closed and completely evacuated as an old bomb was discovered and needed to be put away.

At a walk through the city I was told that, after WW II, the next winter, as the people didn't have enough wood to warm up what was left of their houses, they cut down almost all trees from the 'Tiergarten' park, to make fire with them. So basically most of the trees there are younger than expected.

Also, as a result of the cruel division this city went through, Berlin has now two Opera Houses, two Zoos (one of them, Tierpark, the largest zoo in Europa, was our favourite), two Aquariums... on both sides of the city you can find one... as a reminder of the old times...but also more for us to explore ☺

Even if they have been through some rough times, they honour their past and smartly make the best out of it. Checkpoint Charlie, the most famous crossing point between West Berlin and East Berlin, during the separation time and Cold War period, is now actually one of the most visited and touristic places in Berlin. People go there, visit the Museum across the street, take pictures with the guards dressed as former American and Soviet soldiers and maybe, if the weather is nice, they have a famous East Berlin 'Soft Eis' (soft vanilla ice cream in a comb) and go up in the sky in a huge balloon, to admire the city from above. There is also a DDR Museum in the centre, with objects and stories telling visitors what was like living in East Germany (DDR), in the communist era. I was never curious to visit it, as I had my share of memories from my own childhood in a communist country. If you want, you may also go on a 'Trabi safari', driving an old small East-German car, Trabant, very funny looking for the people today, but the emblem of East German society in the communist times and also full of nice memories for the ones who owned one back in those days, my family included. As I was just a little girl, I remember we were very proud of our German car, even if it was very small and looked more like a toy car.

When driving or walking through the city, you will for sure observe the different looking city pedestrian traffic lights. They all feature the iconic 'Ampelman', now turned into a real city trademark (and a very commercial one, also). Once only in East Berlin, now they are all over the city and in dedicated stores, in red and green, showing you when to stop or cross the streets. We became quite familiar with the Ampelman stores across Berlin, as our kids simply loved to play at the small traffic lights they had inside and devoured the gummy bears they offered to children at the cash desks☺. A few days ago I saw in the centre a few traffic lights where instead of these cute figurines there were eco-friendly messages: 'eat less meat' for red colour and 'go vegan' for green. Quite funny! ☺.

If you have heard stories about the city's past during the Cold War, there is a place for you to visit. The famous 'Spy Bridge' (Glienicke Bridge), across the Havel River, is still in one piece and you can cross it when leaving West Berlin on the way to Potsdam. It is a big green bridge which used to be on the border and one of the places where exchanging prisoners and high-ranking spies from East and West Berlin took place. It is still full of historic flavour and mystery. More commercial though is the Spy museum in the middle of town, with stories and also gadgets used to spy, from those times to modern days, from reality to fictional James Bond movies. There are some interesting facts and things for you to see, but to tell you the truth, I have been there once and I was not terribly impressed. The kids loved it though, they pretended they were real spies, went through infra-red wires and got an inspector personalized ID at the end. Some months ago I saw this very clever add on the Spy Museum. It showed on one hand the difficulties of a former spy 40 or 30 years ago and, on the other hand, the reality we live in today, surrounded by artificial intelligence that easily spy on us, mostly with our own complicity. It makes you think a bit about the present and mostly, about the future of mankind...

Living back in the post-war days must have been difficult for the citizens of Berlin. Mostly for the ones living in the eastern side probably, but also for the others. West Berlin was basically an enclave in the middle of East Germany. The West Berlin citizens went through a complete blockade, when they were totally isolated and had food and other aid packages dropped by special planes from the West Germany mother land. I was told some even received special pay, by the end of the 80's, so they would not leave the city and move somewhere else. To enter or go out of Berlin in those days, you had to go through the border into East Germany. A lady that used to be my German teacher, told me once that she remembered when she was little and went to ski to Austria. They had to wake up around 4 am, go stay in line at the border in order to leave West Berlin and cross into East Germany first, then to West Germany again and after many hours of waiting and driving, finally crossing to Austria, to go to ski. It took a whole tiring day to arrive. Awful... the same destination we were able to reach in less than 7 hours, driving on the modern highways nowadays, with no speed limit on most parts, and of course, no more borders to cross (when you drive from Germany to Austria, there is no formal border crossing, just a shield that signals you entered another country within EU).

The same lady remembered they had relatives on the other side of the wall, in the same city, that they saw only after the Wall was down, in 1989. But she also said that she and her friends had no interest to go cross the city former border to the east, to see the other part of the city, for still many years after 1989. It was a long time until she finally went there, running errands and still not by curiosity. It was mainly the East Berliners who went to the West, searching for a better life and it took a while until the city looked more united and the differences in life-style started to fade a bit. However, as another German lady bluntly told me once, the real rich West Berliners stick to their part of town and rarely mix with the rest. Even these days, they still identify themselves when they talk about their origins, as being from west or east (Germany), as a clear indication of background and sometimes even status.

I can only sympathize with the east- Berliners, as I surely understand the drama they have been through. I was born in Bucharest, the capital of Romania, a former communist country, with a regime far worse than the one in East Germany and all the stories that I have heard about the life of the citizens in the eastern part of Berlin seemed very similar to the reality that I lived in for the first 11 years of my life. Although 1989 meant freedom and a new beginning for all the eastern European countries, including both Romania and DDR (East Germany), it takes time to change mentalities, heal traumas and get back to a normal, decent life. The differences in life standards slowly disappear but some are still present to this day. Some of the scars will remain with you forever and will mark the way you behave and think till the day you die.

Maybe some of the aggressiveness in conduct, reluctance towards foreigners or even nostalgia about those times, especially in older people, all these come from the hardship that the east-Berliners have been through and had to endure for decades and now takes its toll. I cannot imagine how it is to wake up one morning and realize you have been left behind, how it is to understand you are on the 'wrong' side of the Wall and your life will be so different and so much worse than the life other people, maybe even family or friends, will have, just few miles away into freedom. I have read of so many dramas at those horrible times, broken families, people killed just for trying to get to the other side of the Wall... Berlin is full of testimonies of these sad stories, which should be remembered. They are part of its history and they shaped the city as it is today.

Truly, if you take a walk into different parts of town, you can easily see the duality of the city. The west is the ground of fine mansions, nice neighbourhoods, elegantly dressed people, diplomatic residences, boulevards with shiny stores and high-end brands. The centre is modern, full of life, home to the many official and historical iconic buildings, the magnificent Reichstag (German Parliament building and former seat of the Weimar Republic Parliament) with its modern newly built glass dome and roof top, the Chancellery (seat of today's government) and most embassies. It is a mixture of expats and tourists, restaurants and shops, new elegant apartment buildings and also historical monuments, reminders of the old times. Above all there is the famous 368 meter tall TV Tower (Fernsehturm), which is the tallest structure in Germany and one of the tallest in Europe. It was built by the communist regime as a symbol of their power, symbol of the modern city of East Berlin. It is still a symbol now, visited daily and photographed by every tourist. For us it was also special, as we lived closed by and, the minute we could see it, we knew we were close on our way home.

The eastern part of Berlin is more proletarian, the buildings are a constant reminder of the Soviet times, mostly expressionless huge apartment buildings, designed to fit in lots of people in small similar looking apartments. However, after the fall of the Berliner Wall, there were parts of it that emerged and are now considered very trendy and posh. Prenzlauer Berg is one of them. It is a lovely area with nice buildings, some of them old and with a special flavour, small family restaurants at each corner and a vivid active community life.

All these parts of a big city are perfectly connected by a vast infrastructure, a large network of metro lines (U-bahn), urban trains (S-bahn), urban highways, buss and tram lines (trams run only in the eastern part of the city) and, most importantly, 620 kilometres of bicycle lanes. Bikers are everywhere, a bit chaotic on the streets sometimes or even aggressive if you accidently step or walk on their designated lane (so watch out!), but they all seem to adore going everywhere by bike, no matter the weather. You could see ladies in short dresses or men wearing suits (my husband included☺), children with their school bags on... all using these eco-friendly locomotion means. But to my wonder, especially compared to Vienna, no one really wears a helmet on (except for kids, maybe). I was also surprised to find out that, in a country that is a champion in car making, with entire cities supported mostly by the car industry, there are a lot of people, at least in Berlin, who don't own a car, and not because they could not afford it, but because they choose public transport instead. Car sharing is also a very popular solution in the city. Actually driving a car in Berlin has become more and more annoying for the last few years, as you can see lots of speed limitations to just 30 km/h, intended to lower the pollution or noise, on many streets. But Germans love speed, on the many toll-free highways of this country, there is no speed limit on most parts.

Berlin is a city in permanent reconstruction, still… When we arrived, the centre was completely renovated. Potsdamer Platz is a big square in the centre of Berlin, with modern architecture and new buildings fit for the 21st century, that kind of reminded me of New York city, when I first saw them. Only a few concrete blocks from the former Wall and the cubic stone line on the street, following the site of the wall all over the city, are reminders and proofs of a dark era. It is hard to imagine that this large square in the middle of Berlin was completely empty 30 years ago, border between two different worlds. I read that this was the biggest construction site in Europe for several years, around year 2000, until all the buildings there were completed.

There is still enormous potential and empty space for construction in the middle of this big metropole, unlike any other in the whole world. We understood it right away.

But as modern and highly-achieved as the German society is, there are still things that amazed us from the very beginning. We were completely disappointed by the long time it took us to get a TV cable contract and an internet provider, also the low-speed internet when we finally got any, or the complete lack of politeness and efficiency of any phone operator, whenever we had a problem and called them for help. To me it was a real ordeal anytime I had to make a call to signal a problem... most of the time I would ask my husband to do it, anyway... as his German was far better and he is also a more relaxed and understanding person than I am. But with all his understanding, he soon reached his limits, too, when talking to a bank operator or otherwise. I guess working by standard procedures is great, but not when you can't think freely and 'outside the box' anymore and respond quickly and properly to a specific new situation. Because of all these times, we had a joke, my husband and I, as I would always ask him to make these calls 'because he speaks German'... he always said he remembered how 'he was a prince' in Romania, not having to deal with any of these ☺ ...

Getting our diplomatic IDs and medical insurance cards also took a while, but we eventually got them, after about a month of waiting for each. Surprisingly, I got my new German driving license (my old one was about to expire) in record time though...but that was maybe partially because there was a specially designated diplomatic office for it...?

Once we settled in, we started our everyday life in the new city of residence. We decided to use our free time to discover Berlin and its surroundings. One of the first places we visited was Potsdam. It is about 30 minutes away from Berlin, capital of Brandenburg district ('land' in German). It is extremely beautiful and we fell in love with it in an instant. It used to be the summer residence of the Kaisers (Prussian kings). The palace, Sanssouci, is a marvellous, rococo style architecture jewel and considered a rival to the equally famous French palace

Versailles. It is surrounded by large gardens full of flowers. The name, 'Sanssouci' means in French 'no worries'… a perfectly chosen name for this beautiful location, where time stood still. Take a walk on the alleys in the garden and you will reach the other palace, the 'New Palace', built later but larger and in a different style. They are both gorgeous and I strongly recommend not to miss a visit there, when in Berlin.

The fact that our first trip was to Potsdam was a wise choice. Of course, it was recommended by my husband's colleagues from the Embassy. They obviously knew it better. For us it was even more beautiful as it reminded us of the Viennese days, of the splendour and grandeur of the Schönbrunn Palace in Vienna and its lovely gardens with perfectly cut grass and lots of flowers. We loved Sanssouci and spent many weekends there. Whenever we had guests we took them to visit it.

In Potsdam, which also has a picturesque city centre, with nice old but renovated buildings, you can also visit the Cecilienhof palace. It is the last palace built by the House of Hohenzollern (that ruled in Prussia and also Romania). It has a quite unique appearance comparing with the other palaces in Potsdam, as it was built in an English Tudor style. It is now a hotel but it is mostly visited and remembered for its historic importance: it was the location for the Potsdam Conference in 1945, at the end of World War II, where unfortunately, the future division of Europe, between West and East, was decided. The powerful leaders of United States, United Kingdom and Soviet Union, Truman, Churchill and Stalin, set at a table overlooking the garden and the lake and decided the division of Germany and Europe into democratic and communist countries. For me, coming from Romania who was left behind the 'Iron Curtain' for almost 50 years because of those decisions, it was extremely emotional to visit it for the first time. Just the thought that, with a simple pen in their hands, three people decided in a few hours the destiny and misery of millions, still makes me sad.

I will always keep in mind all the stories that my grandpa, a former major in the Romanian Army and later prisoner of war in Germany and political prisoner in Soviet Union, told me when I was just a little girl. All those horrors of war and post war tragedy that millions of people had to face because of the madness and decisions of a few... these are things that should never be forgotten and never repeated! Everybody should learn and remember the history lessons and never allow for the same mistakes to be made again.

Observing the Berliners for the last 4 years, it seems to me a bit odd that the proverbial attention to details, that is considered the basis of Germany's success, is not something you can find everywhere and in everyday life in Berlin. The streets are not always very clean, the grass is almost never cut and the bushes are left to grow wild. The leaves that fall from the trees in autumn are left on the streets and sidewalks until almost end of November and only when there are no more leaves to fall, they are finally swept away... maybe it is out of practical, economical reasons, but it still feels a bit strange... and annoying to walk and sometimes have you feet fully covered in brown leaves.

Also their unique sense of style amazed me from the very beginning and it still does today. They seem to have a real adversity to showing off. Berliners hate shiny clothes, big logos and, except for only one or two big famous stores in town, I could never find stylish elegant shoes. Only comfortable but ugly looking ones. They like to dress up in a practical but completely unfashionable way. Summers are for wearing slippers almost everywhere (the famous Birkenstock sandals mostly). I understood later that it is not easy to wear high heels in Berlin... by paying a high price, I might add ... Because of the nature of the majority of Berlin's sidewalks, which are mostly paved with sharp-cut cubic stones, I have destroyed several pairs of gorgeous stilettos, getting them stuck between stones and scratching their thin heels irreparably. My heart hurts ☺...

Berliners are generally very modest in appearance, even the richest ones don't like to wear many jewellery. I am not 100% sure, but I suppose part of this attitude comes from their religion. Germans are mostly Christians (only 5% of population believes in Islam, population mostly of foreign background). The northern part of Germany is mainly protestant and the south is in majority catholic. If you enter and compare churches, you will see that the protestant ones are less luxurious and less decorated, more modest in appearance, opposite to the catholic ones. So maybe this inspired also the people's attitude and simple way of life.

I will always remember the first day of school when we went together with the whole family to celebrate the beginning of school time for our children, especially for our youngest, a first grader. Starting school is considered a big event in Germany and it is celebrated by the whole family, parents, and grandparents. All first graders will get a big 'Schultüte', which is a large cone made out of paper or cardboard and filled with candies, toys and school material by the parents. It is meant to be a memorable day for the children. It is often celebrated at restaurants, after school ceremonies are over. Although a very festive and important occasion, we still felt awkward when we discovered we were completely overdressed, comparing to the other participants. I understood then that the notion of 'elegance' is completely differently perceived and interpreted in Berlin, by the locals.

Of course, when participating in diplomatic events, I found again the same sense of fashion and definition of style that I was familiar with, from our days in Vienna. Elegant ladies, feminine dresses, high heel shoes and sophisticated hairstyles, they were all there, within these closed circles. But definitely difficult to be found on the streets of Berlin.

During the time I lived in Germany, I was lucky enough to be part of few fashion shows and runways of some luxury local brands. They all testified that most of their clients came from outside Germany, mostly from Asia. The Asian clients seem to appreciate and value more the 'niche' brands, not so popular and well known to the general public, but very expensive and highly exclusivist. Whenever you want to find nice and high quality shoes or clothes, go to KaDeWe, the second largest department store in Europe (after Harrods in London). I always enjoyed going there, although in the western part of town, so not really walking distance from our house. Closer, on the legendary Friedrichstrasse, I often went to Galleries Lafayette, the German branch of the famous Parisian store, where, besides high-end brand clothing, you could also find one of the best and tastiest pastry-shops in the city, with my favorite 'eclairs'. Unfortunately I just read that they are thinking of leaving this location, as it is probably not that profitable anymore... However, Friedrichstrasse is also home to some other famous German brands, like Escada or Karl Lagerfeld. I was impressed by people's tribute to the talented designer on the news of his death. You could see lots of white flowers at the shop window, for days in a row. When speaking of German brands, Aigner is one that I like. The company based in Munich designs and manufactures high- quality leather bags and accessories mostly. Their style is elegant and the products fit for any occasion. I had the opportunity to participate in a special presentation of the brand, with one of their leather masters explaining the whole production process to us, emphasizing on the great attention they pay to details, quality of leather and exquisite handcraft. I admit I became a loyal customer after that day ☺

I adored also the feminine dresses from Hallhuber or the refined products from Maisonnoée, a Berlin-based high-quality fashion brand that I was introduced to. I always wondered though why I could rarely see any of those beautiful clothes from stores on Berlin's streets... It made me many times regret Vienna and its elegance.

Another thing that made me nostalgic about our Viennese days was the general aggressiveness of people on the streets, both in language and attitude. I was certainly not used to it, nor prepared. Romanians are traditionally very kind and helpful towards foreigners and so were the Austrians. Not the same story in Berlin. Strangers on the street would stop and talk to you in a loud superior voice, especially once they figured out you don't speak proper native German, some would be really rude, argue with you for the smallest reasons or no reason at all and even shout at you with a total lack of politeness if you accidentally did not talk to them with 'SIE' (most formal pronoun), to which they are veeeeeeery sensitive. They seemed to resent anyone not speaking their language properly and rarely saw any smiling face. Everything seemed pretty gloomy for the first few months.

It took a long time to finally meet some nice locals, mostly parents of children from school or spouses of German diplomats. Also some of our neighbours eventually started talking to us and making nice conversation, especially after I helped few times with their mail or accepted their packages from currier in their absence. But it took a while!

Even when going to the doctor, I remember there was this lady doctor that never shook hands with me, motivating every time she was sick or had a flu... speaking of doctors, most of the ones we've seen seemed quite distant, emotionally detached, with a low level of compassion towards the patients. Maybe it was just in our opinion, but we decided then to look for doctors, mainly other than Germans, to go to, in order to be greeted with a warmer approach, more comfortable to us and the children. Even so, the waiting time for any medical appointment was long and some doctors asked for appointments even when it was something quite urgent...I wonder how was it possible to figure out weeks in advance that my daughter would have a swollen eye or a skin rush all of a sudden or that I will have stuffy ears...? And when you finally got to see a doctor, they would recommend, most of the times, that you just wait for few days to see if the problem goes away by itself and, if not, return for more treatment. I know people who were fined for calling the ambulance, for what they thought was an emergency case, but it was not considered so. You can get almost no pills from the pharmacy without a doctor prescription. So, every summer when we were visiting our family and friends in Romania, we were also refilling our stock of 'just in case' medicines, for the next year abroad.

Vaccination is a different thing, though. They recommend that all children should be immunized, at least with the minimum mandatory vaccines, before entering school. I remember they asked sometimes for the vaccination card of my children, before going on school trips. You may even be fined if the kids don't have the mandatory ones done.

However, I think their medical system is superior to many in Europe, with world-renowned centres of excellence.

Back to my everyday life, eventually I managed to discover the real Berliners and to understand their way of behaving. I guess that not knowing anybody in the city when we originally moved, forced us indirectly to interact more with the locals and helped us to understand the Berlin society more profoundly. Not everybody can be open and friendly from the very beginning. Berliners are certainly not. They do not open their hearts, nor their homes to anybody right away. But, once you start to know them, you see that they have quite a good sense of humour, they can be trusty, loyal people. Especially the younger generation is more open and friendly towards foreigners.

Generally, they are taught from childhood to be fair and tell the truth, even if it is blunt and painful sometimes. They do everything by the book, they are taught to follow rules and procedures and maybe this is the key to Germany's success. Germany has, after all, the largest economy in Europe, they produce much more than they spend, they seem to have a constant budget surplus, comforting, of course, in times of economic crisis. With their more than 80 million people, they are also the largest market within the European Union and they manage to have, in the same time, one of the lowest unemployment rates in the Union. This should give them reasons to relax a bit... but it is not in their nature, I suppose. I learned that German companies are highly hierarchical, rule-oriented, respecting procedures and long-term planning. Managers usually remain with a firm for many years, sometimes until retirement, they are often interested in reaching consensus and a good work-environment, not too personal though, they don't like price-based competition and emphasize on the quality of German products. It seems as any German employee has a specialization, graduated a qualifying course, or has a diploma, whether from university or not. I know even shop assistants have to attend long term courses before starting their job.

Once they are hired, after an initial six- month test period, they often get long-term contracts, highly secure for employees' rights, as Germans are not really work-addicts, like other nations, appreciating their free time more than anything else.

Germany is a global top political player but also a master of using its soft-power tools, ranking second globally, especially through Education and Enterprise global index. Magnetic metropoles like Berlin and Hamburg have helped Germany's good name rise as well as the proverbial high-quality of German products.

Although a very progressive and modern society, Germany has a low women employment rate and a relatively high gender pay gap. Most of the women I have met at my kids' school were not working full time or not working at all. They were raising their kids, taking care of their families and enjoying life.

Berlin is recognized as a city with a mood for life, a Bohemian town, 'multikulti' as they would describe it, much more relaxed than other German cities.

Berliners don't appreciate anything too shrill but they pride themselves on the diversity of this city, they value their privacy but boast on the freedom of expression. They don't care how you dress or even if you are dressed at all, as there are plenty of places specially reserved for staying naked, even in public parks or on the beach ('FKK' areas). No matter how eccentric you are, you will find your place in Berlin for sure and you will be able to assert your opinions freely.

I have never seen another city with so many rallies, on any cause, from the rights of LGBTQ community to cheap housing, more bike lanes (although plenty), family rights, healthy nutrition and so on... for us it was annoying sometimes to have all those blocked streets, and so often… but they all seemed happy to participate, no matter the outcome.

Also Berlin is the city of many festivals, sports and big cultural street events, most of them free of charge. It is the 'Karnaval der Kulturen' (Cultural Carnival), each year during the Whit Sunday public holiday, with food and costumes from all over the world, the Festival of Lights, in October, with the most iconic buildings in the city wonderfully illuminated or the 'Open Air' festival in Gendarmenmarkt. 'Staatsoper für alle' ('State Opera for Everyone') is an annual classical concert on a temporary stage in front of the State Opera house in Bebelplatz, Berlin-Mitte, highly popular among both Berliners and tourists. By the way, did you know that Berlin State Opera was the first in Europe to open to the general public?

The famous 'Berlin Marathon' is one of the biggest sport events in the world and a highlight every September, attended also, to our pride and joy, by our own family's athlete, for every year of our Berlin adventure. The Berlinale, Berlin's famous international film festival since 1978 and one of the "Big Three", alongside the Venice Film Festival and Cannes Film Festival, attracts each February lots of big cinema stars, film directors and the largest public audience of any annual film festival. Up to 400 films are shown in several sections each year and the 'Golden Bear' is a much-wanted prize among professionals. I am proud to say that it was won also by Romanian artists, the latest in 2018 ('Touch me not' by Adina Pintilie).

Every winter the city turns magical as the Advent Christmas markets open all over the city. It is basically one at each corner or in any bigger square. My favorite was always the one in Gendarmenmarkt. I found it very elegant, traditional and authentic, maybe even more than the more famous one, in front of the City Hall in Vienna. They also last a bit longer than the Viennese ones (which close exactly on December 24th). Because of the huge crowds that all these Christmas markets attract each year, unfortunately they became also a target for terrorists. They are all now carefully guarded and protected by huge concrete blocks and strong fences, but back in 2016, before all these security measures, a tragedy stroke. It was a peaceful December evening when a truck was deliberately driven into the jolly crowds of locals and tourists, at the Christmas market in Breitscheidplatz, a major public square in the inner city, in front of Kaiser Wilhelm Memorial Church. Twelve people were killed and many injured. It was the most horrific terrorist attack in Germany in recent years and it happened in a place that I had visited only two days before. It was in the western part of the city, so not exactly close to our home, but one of the most popular attractions every winter, during Advent time. We immediately let everyone from back home know we were OK. My father joked though, saying that, because this tragic event had happened later in the evening, he was not worried at all, as he was pretty sure we were already in bed at the time of the attack. Sometimes it's good to have small kids with strict bed time curfew, I guess ☺

The New Year is celebrated with great joy in Berlin, in front of the Brandenburg Gate, with a big concert attended by thousands of spectators, who usually come hours in advance, to catch a place in front. At midnight the fireworks conquer the sky of the city in a magical show of lights. I have never seen so many fireworks on sky at the same time anywhere else. Berlin definitely loves fireworks!

On the occasion of the 'Unity day'- Germany's National day, each year on October 3rd, one of the largest boulevards in Berlin, '17 Juni' is completely closed for traffic and opens up to pedestrian celebration, with live music on big stages and lots of traditional German food.

When it comes to traditional food, I have to say Germans, as much as Austrians, love pork. They have lots of meat specialties that go perfectly with a cold beer, or two... The famous 'curry wurst mit pommes' is the trade-mark local food in Berlin since 1949. It is basically a grilled sausage with ketchup, curry powder and French fries aside, which you can serve at any corner of any street in the city. Berlin is also proud to have invented and make the best 'Döner kebab' (a Turkish dish originally made by the first Turkish migrants who came to Berlin after the WW II). A warm sandwich with bread, thin slices of meat cut from a vertical, special type of rotisserie, cabbage, onion, tomatoes, spices and a special sauce that binds all the ingredients... It makes the delight of the Berliners and all tourists. For vegetarians there is an alternative with Haloumi, a special tasty grilled cheese, instead of meat. 'Mustafa Kebab' is the name that you will probably find in most of the tourists' reviews about the famous Berliner döner kebab. It is considered to be the best in the city. It is incredible how, although a small shop in a not very inviting area, can attract so many gourmets every day, sitting sometimes up to half an hour or more in line, just to have one. We tried it once and, I must confess, it didn't seem that special to us... maybe we are not the right ones to decide...

But when we talk about ice cream and chocolate... we are experts ☺ ... so, if you come to Berlin, please stop by 'Whoop Whoop' store on Rosenthaler Strasse for their special and insanely creamy ice cream, made directly in front of you using liquid nitrogen technology. If you are a chocolate lover, go to Rausch in Gendarmenmarkt for the best chocolate and best chocolate cakes in town or, if you want to have some fun and taste some good chocolate in the same time, go around the corner, to Ritter Sport store, where you can design your own mix for a signature chocolate bar. A good chocolate and definitely the best chai-latte in town will wait for you at Berliner Kaffeerosterei, in the western part of the city. I confess that I became totally addicted to it after the first time I have been there and tried it in the lovely surroundings of their library room.

Berlin has a 'Strawberries time', a 'Pumpkin time' or 'Asparagus time', when it seems that any restaurant serves dishes with these seasonal products. But, above all, potatoes are kings here. Everybody loves potatoes and eats them with everything. Potato salad is something that they can serve with any dish, on any occasion. I remember my surprise and amusement when I was asking a German friend of mine about traditional dishes for Christmas or Easter and

'Potato salad' always came first on the list. Ironically I read a story about how potatoes were originally introduced to the German population and how they were seen as poisonous at first. Only from the 19th century they became the most popular 'new food' in Europe and its many advantages were finally acknowledged. Potatoes are cheap, they can be stored easily and for a long time and they keep hunger away. After all, Berlin has known terrible periods of famine, so it's no wonder that potato salad still appears so often on the menu.

Berlin is nowadays a 'green' city. In reality and also in politics ('Die Grünen', meaning 'The Greens', is a German party with many followers in Berlin). In fact the whole Germany is a big champion when it comes to renewable energy sources, they plan to 'go green' completely by 2050. Everywhere you travel in the country you see thousands of tall windmills, with their white silhouettes dominating the landscape. There is not one shop that will give you a plastic bag for free, most don't even sell plastic bags at all. They try to cut down on anything made out of plastic, in fact. All plastic bottles are sold against an additional 25 cents fee, which you can get back once you return the bottle to any supermarket in town. They have a lot of time especially allocated in school for discussions on that theme. No wonder that the 'Friday is for Future' movement caught so well in Berlin. The string of demonstrations, initiated by the Swedish school girl Greta Thunberg, with young students participating every Friday, together with their teachers, in front of the iconic Brandenburg Gate, is meant to signal about climate change and demand immediate actions to prevent irreparable changes that will affect generations to come. My children also participated, together with their classes, and, although one might question the real immediate results of such actions, I am sure that raising awareness of such reality is equally important. It also helps raising responsible and involved citizens for tomorrow.

German education system pays special attention to raising good and responsible adults, with highly developed civic sense, actively involved in the life and destiny of their city and their country. They are taught how voting system works and what elections are good for, they learn the first steps of democracy from elementary school. They have school elections that they organize and participate in, they are encouraged to have ideas and not be afraid to tell them out loud.

Berliners also teach their children a lot of practical things in school. Every third grader will learn to swim, as they have swimming lessons once a week, and every fourth grader will learn to ride a bike on public roads, they also have gardening clubs and recycling workshops in schools. In order to raise money for their class trips and also to understand the real value of money, they make and sell cupcakes, lemonade, they donate and sell their used toys and books or have fund raising sports events. They are taught about human rights, tolerance and compassion.

At early age children are very receptive and they learn and remember everything very fast. They have a curiosity and need to discover new things all the time. I know this from my own children but also from others that I had the privilege to meet in Berlin. I was invited a few times to local kindergartens in the city to talk about Romania, my native country. I was really impressed by the warmth they all greeted me with and the genuine interest these small kids showed. I told them a short funny story written by one of our famous writers, Ion Creanga, about a clever fox and a bear and the importance of thinking before acting on an impulse. We then talked about countries, languages and people from different parts of the world, the importance of acceptance and friendship between individuals, no matter what country they come from. I treasure those meetings and I am happy and grateful I've done it.

After the first few difficult months in Berlin, we finally started to enjoy the city and feel comfortable and 'at home'. Berlin is beautiful, once you really discover it. It is one of the greenest cities on Earth, every street is tree lined and lots of forests are to be found inside and around the city. I especially enjoyed the beautiful Japanese cherry trees with their gorgeous pink small flowers, in full blossom every spring. Berlin got them as a present from the Japanese government, after the fall of the Berlin Wall and they were mostly planted on the former border line between the two parts of the city. They are really wonderful, a true delight to anyone's eye. I absolutely have to also mention the divine smell of linden trees, which filled the air in late May and June every year. Linden trees are everywhere in the city, they even have one of the largest boulevards named after them, 'Unter den Linden' (Under the linden trees). We also went for long walks in Grunewald, in the borough of Charlottenburg-Wilmersdorf, a deep large forest area in Berlin. It is really incredible how you can drive for only few kilometres and get to this beautiful place, where you already feel like you are at the mountains, smelling the fresh air under the trees and maybe taking a deep in the Teufelssee (in English: Devil's Lake), a glacial lake in the middle of the forest. Because of all this rich beautiful nature in the city, Berlin is also full of small animals, living their peaceful and undisturbed lives among humans. We could see lots of squirrels around our house, even o fox visited us on the tennis court, one evening (Berlin is full of foxes and they are protected in the city).

I remember I saw this very funny video of a string of ducks waiting for the green light to pass the street, in another German town. Or I read last year about a story, which later made international headlines, about a fat rat that got stuck in the lid of a sewer canal and was rescued by German firefighters. In order to reduce the number of rats and mice in the city, crows are protected by law (they feed on rats and mice). Germans care about wild life and protect its balance.

In general, Berlin is full of forests, lakes and even two rivers that run through, Spree and Havel, which you can cruise on for hours with larger or small ranted boats, floating houses or paddle boats. The outskirts of the city are also a natural paradise for bikers, swimmers or sailors. Most of the lakes have sandy beaches, ready for summer time fun and relaxation. We especially loved going to Müggelsee, one of the largest lakes in Berlin, where we would spend lovely days with the whole family. It is a big lake but it is not very deep, so it was perfect for families, even with small children, and it was warm enough for a good swim or for a standup paddle boarding session. It is located in the eastern part of Berlin while the westerners have Wannsee lake, much deeper but equally popular with the locals. I loved going to the Wansee terrace in summer, having a cold drink or ice cream on the terrace overlooking the lake, admiring all the boats and windsurfers. What a view...just beautiful! My kids also adored Orankesee, a much smaller lake, but with a water slide and sandy beach, perfect for a day of fun in the middle of Berlin, in summer time.

When the weather was still cold, we sometimes went to Tropical Islands, just an- hour drive away from Berlin. It is a wonderful tropical theme park, largest indoor water park in the world, housed in a former airship hangar (known as the Aerium), and the third biggest free-standing hall in the world. With a constant indoor air temperature of 26 ° Celsius, this great human-made paradise is home to the biggest indoor rainforest in the world, a beach, many tropical plants and a large number of swimming pools, water slides, bars and restaurants. You can even fly around in a hot air balloon!

When autumn comes, all forests around Berlin turn into a true symphony of colours, all shades of brown and yellow, caressed by gentle September sunshine. It is as if a talented painter decided to make his own masterpiece on the streets of the city.

Speaking of masterpieces, Berlin is one of the greatest cities when it comes to museums. From fine pieces of classical or contemporary painting to ancient artefacts, you can find them all here. The Museum Island is place to some of the most visited world class museums. 'Pergamon Museum' is one of the most popular attractions in Berlin, the most visited museum in the city and one of the most visited in whole Germany, hosting the impressive Ishtar Gate of Babylon, partly with its original colors, the Market Gate of Miletus, completely reconstructed from its ruins found in Anatolia or the Pergamon Altar. My personal favorite museum remains 'Neues Museum', Berlin's museum of ancient Egypt, home to the famous bust of queen Nefertiti and many other relics from those times. If you want to visit any of these museums though, you should prepare yourself for long waiting hours, especially in summer time. Close to the museum island you may visit also the German Historical museum, hosted in one of the oldest buildings on Unter den Linden Boulevard, a beautiful baroque style building. The Jewish museum is also very popular, not far away, in the middle of Berlin. Museum of Technology was one of my kids' favorite, also Science Center Spectrum, with lots of interactive experiment stations and interesting things to discover. Most of the museums have free entry for children or at least reduced rates. I heard that there is even a discussion nowadays about a free- admission Sunday to everybody, once a month. All to increase the general accessibility to the many museums in town. I read somewhere that Berlin has more museums than rainy days. There are 180 museums in Berlin and less than 110 rainy days on average per year... hmmm... that's interesting, I really thought there were more rainy days... it certainly seems like it...

Before we moved to Berlin, a lot of people had warned us about the weather. So we really expected the worst of it. It rains a lot, it is true. And it is windy sometimes. It rarely snows in winters and it is neither too cold, nor to hot in summers, which is good. You can easily go through almost all four seasons in one day, as weather can change in a matter of hours dramatically. Anyway, during our stay in Berlin, we got to experience (in 2018 and 2019) the hottest summers ever recorded in Berlin. People are certainly not used to extreme temperatures and all city seemed to melt down at 35 to even 42(!) degrees Celsius. But generally the summer temperatures are milder, little over 20 degrees. We come from Bucharest, Romania's capital, with hot and dry long summers, with often temperatures above 30 degrees, so we love good hot weather. I especially missed the sunny days, as they are quite scarce in Berlin. As a totally sun-dependent person, I found myself always craving for sunshine in the city and I was always looking forward to the next sunny day. There were entire months when you barely saw the sun... always cloudy sky above your head. This can easily cause depressions and I learned Berliners have such problems often. The fact that in winter time it usually got dark around 3.30 p.m. and stayed this way until around 8 a.m. the next day, didn't help too much either. Long cold nights can make you feel blue... It happened to me, too... Although busy and active with the kids and diplomatic events, life in Berlin was pretty lonely for me, at least the first year... the first winter was particularly difficult... and winter gloomy weather roughly lasts from end September till April... While my husband was at work and the kids in school, there were many days when I had hardly anyone to talk to the whole day long. I had no friends, no family, just a small circle of diplomatic spouses that I would meet from time to time, most of them going through the same feelings like myself. Going out in the cold rain or winter windy weather didn't seem too appealing most days either. So I started to feel a bit low and slightly slipped to depression. Maybe it seems strange or impossible that someone in my position, which looks idyllic to most, would experience these feelings or suffer from depression. I was sad and very emotional, especially during daytime, when I was alone, I couldn't sleep well at night, wake up every night around 2 or 3 a.m. and could not go back to sleep.

Coming to the age of forty had its share, too. I think it is usually around this age when you start to become more aware of your own mortality, you start questioning your purpose in life and you also evaluate it: what you have accomplished so far, what dreams you had and what was fulfilled of them, what you are going to do next. You're starting to realize very acutely the fast and irreversible passage of time, you see your children grow up so fast, no babies anymore... You're starting to realize there's no time or possibility for many of the things you had in mind at 20 and that you have to look more realistically to the future ahead. I had all these inner questions about my meaning, my legacy... maybe this book is also part of this inner struggle, to leave something more behind...in written form ☺

Because of all my swinging blue moods, I figured out something was wrong with me and went to see a therapist. After some random tests, she concluded there was nothing too serious, just a mild condition for the moment, but I certainly needed to make some changes fast, so that it wouldn't get serious. She strongly recommended that I should increase my social life, as she explained to me that anyone needs, besides the support of a loving family, which I fully had, the feeling of BELONGING to a group, other than the immediate loved ones. We all need to feel useful, to be involved in something and to have our own activities and projects outside our own home environment and close circle of acquaintances. She also admitted it was not unusual for someone in my position to have these feelings and that she'd met often other people, living the expat lifestyle, with similar problems and difficulties. She recommended long walks, staying outside as much as possible, new activities and having a wider social circle, if possible. The truth is that I met lots of new interesting people every week, but I had no real connection to any, I made no new friends in Berlin and lacked the warmth of my old friends back home. I badly needed to do something outside my standard every day schedule. In fact that is what I had desired from the very beginning. After the wonderful experience I had had in Vienna, working at the United Nations Women's Guild, I had started to look for some similar involvement from the very first week of my life in Germany. To my great disappointment, although I had sent hundreds of resumes and emails to lots of NGOs based in Berlin, offering my volunteer contribution, experience and expertise, I got no reply. I still cannot understand: how can somebody turn down anyone's offer for free help?!...

My luck turned around one day, when, while attending a certificate program in Cultural Diplomacy and International Relations, that I had enrolled and completed later, I met this nice lady, a representative of UNICEF Berlin. I told her about me and my previous experience in NGOs and she invited me to one of their meetings. In fact, there was a new international volunteer group, mainly with English speaking people from Berlin area, which seemed perfect for me. I cannot tell you how anxiously I waited for that first meeting… and that was the start of my UNICEF journey, which still continues today. I found a very nice group of young people, mostly international students, being eager to help and do something worthy in their spare time. We had meetings twice a month and organized events mainly for the English speaking community in Berlin (which is quite large). And so I started organizing charity concerts, school and kindergarten presentations and workshops and participated in all other sorts of events, mainly designed to raise awareness about UNICEF's work in Germany and around the world. UNICEF may be the most well-known children foundation on earth but I discovered that most people aren't fully aware of the scale and professionalism of its work round the clock. It is sometimes inconceivable how little money can make a real difference in a child's life far away and how some small act of kindness and compassion can turn somebody's fate for the better. I must admit that, at first, I did not get the same kind of satisfaction out of my work, as when I was working in Vienna, and that is especially because, in the case of my work at UNICEF, I could not immediately see the results of it, I could not really measure the amount of money that I raised after one project or event and I could not see the direct impact of it in a community that needed it badly. I couldn't choose where the raised money went, to which specific cause. But in time, I realized our work mattered and made a difference somewhere, maybe on another continent, that with the money we raised, some poor children had something to eat for few days, were maybe immunized against some deadly virus or had clean water to drink... and it was all worth it, believe me! The emotional rewards that you get from these activities are priceless!

I always enjoy the adrenaline of a project's deadline, the preparations that come with it and the anticipation of the results. Whenever possible, I tried to involve my kids into it as well and I am proud that they free-willingly participated in some of our group activities and helped as much as they could. I always wanted them to appreciate the good life they live and to be fully aware of the cruel reality that many people and, sadly, children have to face every day on this planet, not having any guilt for being born in a less developed geographical area. In order to raise good, involved citizens for tomorrow, you have to expose them to the reality of today... I also think that you always have to be grateful for the privileged life you have and never forget to help others less fortunate, whenever and however you feel possible. Diplomatic life is good and privileged, no doubt about it... and it can easily make you lose contact with reality and ordinary life, so it's important to keep your feet on the ground all the time... stay humble and grateful for your life, as a professor once told me ...

Back to our daily life, in order to feel more comfortable, we developed our own family routines: Friday was 'pizza day', on weekends we ate fish, every Sunday morning we played tennis, Wednesday evening was 'cinema night'... These routines give you a sense of continuance that will help and soften the shock of moving so often... My kids also enjoyed going to the basketball games of Alba Berlin with their father on evenings sometimes, or to the legendary Olympiastadion to see Herta (Berlin's football team) play.

Whenever we had time we also travelled away from Berlin. Traditionally, diplomatic holidays are quite long, comparing to other professions. Diplomats usually have six weeks of holiday or even more, depending on their job destination. So, plenty of time to explore our country of residency or further destinations.

We did a lot of weekend trips in Germany, we enjoyed the lovely town of Quedlinburg, dating back from the 9th century and close to the Harz Mountains. We also loved our trips to the Saxon Switzerland, two hours away from Berlin. It is a rocky climbing national park, overlooking the Elbe River. It is mainly made up of high pointed rocks, formed by water erosion millions of years ago. The view from the top is absolutely spectacular, Bastei being its most famous rock (194 m above the river), with an equally famous bridge (remember the movie 'Grand Budapest Hotel'?). Not far from it, you can also visit the porcelain factory in Meissen, together with the lovely Albrechtsburg Castle, up on a hill.

Dresden is one of the most beautiful cities in Germany in my opinion, also not far from Berlin. It is a baroque and rococo style jewel, almost completely destroyed during the WW II but now reconstructed.

Driving further south, you can go to Rothenburg ob der Tauber, a small but picturesque medieval village or to Nürnberg (Nuremberg), 'the most German of German cities' as they call it, home to the famous Museum of Toys and also a spectacular Christmas market. Munchen (Munich), Bavaria's capital and a beautiful rich city in South Germany, is also one of my favourites. It is worldwide famous for its traditional craft beer festival, Oktoberfest, every year in late September, attracting millions of tourists with its cheerful atmosphere, like no other. I first visited Munchen when I was a student and fell in love with its beautiful City Hall grand building (Rathaus) and the famous 'Glockenspiel', a special program of bells and moving figurines, having their show few times a day, to the admiration and joy of tourists from all over the world.

We went through the city of Munich every winter, while driving to Garmisch- Partenkirchen for our ski holiday, which is just an hour away from the big Bavarian city. This is the most famous German ski resort, home to an important World Cup ski race and also one of the hosts for the Four Trampolines Tournament, each winter. It is a beautiful traditional little town, close to the Austrian border, at the feet of the highest mountain peak in Germany, the Zugspitze (2962 m). Although it has now one of the most modern and big cable cars in Europe, you can still reach the top of the mountain by an old train, the Bavarian 'Zugspitzbahn', one of the only four rack railways still working in Germany. It goes up in about half an hour from the last stop, most of this time going through a narrow tunnel carved into the mountain. Once you reach the top, the view is absolutely breathtaking. On one side you are in Germany and on the other, on Austrian soil. We enjoyed our time there, every winter, we liked the Bavarian hospitality, their beer and traditional food, the mountains, the people, the town.

Not far from Garmisch we also visited once the charming village of Mittenwald, rated as one of the most beautiful little villages in Bavaria, with its colourful painted houses at the feet of the Alps. It is also known for its long history of violin-making.

But if you want to slip into a fairytale, you have to go visit the Neuschwanstein Castle, up on a hill above the village of Hohenschwangau, southeast Bavaria. It is a beautiful Romanesque palace and an immense tourist attraction, with more than 1.3 million visitors every year (more than 61 million people have visited it so far). It is said to have been the inspiration for the famous Disney castles.

From Berlin we also travelled up north, especially in summer time. We visited Hamburg and we instantly fell in love with it. It has a more aristocratic look and you can smell elegance (if it only could be smelt) with any step you take into this Hanseatic city, the second largest city in Germany (1.8 million people). I especially admired the harbor (one of the biggest in Europe), all its waterways and many canals that run through the city and the new Opera house, the Elbphilharmonie, with its impressive modern design and great acoustic. For night life 18+, there is nothing better than St. Pauli area, vivid and merry.

Also up north we discovered Germany's most beautiful castle, in my opinion, Schwerin Castle. It is a big fairytale-like castle, settled on the lake Schwerin, being today the center of power in Mecklenburg-Vorpommern and the seat of local Parliament. Part of the castle is a museum and may be visited, along with its beautiful gardens. I remember we spent a lovely day there.

We definitely could not live for few years in Germany and not go to the Baltic Sea. It is situated north-east and, although the water was not as warm as we would have liked, we enjoyed its clarity and the fine white sandy beaches, filled with trademark beach chairs, with their white and blue striped canvas. There is a certain flavor to this scenery. Usedom island, Heringsdorf, Rostock or Travemünde are places at the Baltic Sea that are worth visiting, for sure. Close to Travemünde is the UNESCO World Heritage Site and leading city of the Hanseatic League, Lübeck, with its extensive brick Gothic architecture and the best marzipan in the world, from the famous Niederegger company.

With Berlin being so close to the border, we had the opportunity to also explore the neighbour countries. So we've easily travelled to the Check Republic and visited old Prague. We drove to Poland to see the world's tallest Christ statue (taller than the more famous one in Rio, Brazil) in the town of Swiebodzin. We were totally impressed by the grandeur of this construction and also added a personal reminder to our visit there: it is in front of the Christ statue where my son lost his first milk tooth ☺

Driving from Berlin we discovered, on our way to Amsterdam (the Netherlands), the beautiful town of Münster, considered to be the cultural center of the Westphalia region. Also, driving west, one should not miss Hanover, Bremen, Düsseldorf nor Cologne, with its impressive Catholic cathedral, a world heritage site.

Moving to Berlin meant a slight change in our diplomatic life, which seemed more alert, with lots of important events happening all the time, demanding presence and attention. During our stay here, Romania had the rotating Presidency of the European Union for the first time since its accession in 2007. There were also Romanian general and presidential elections, very delicate to organize, due to the impressive size of the Romanian community in Germany (around 800,000 people, the third largest) and the small number of human resources directly involved.

From presenting the letters of accreditation of any new ambassador to the President (the president greets the new ambassador, his wife and a small number of diplomats, all festively dressed to the occasion , at the presidential Bellevue Palace) to other first-rate events, they all seemed to be at a much higher level and protocol.

Berlin is one of the most important capitals in the world, politically speaking... as proof, the large number of high-ranking officials and personalities that regularly came to Berlin.

Barack Obama, the 44th president of the United States visited Berlin three times, twice during our stay in the city. He is still highly popular in Germany and the speech he gave near the iconic Brandenburg Gate, city's greatest symbol, in front of a big crowd in 2013, is memorable. As he took off his jacket, to be more 'informal among friends', he spoke, with his well-recognized oratorical talent, about the importance of human tolerance, freedom and democracy in today's world, a globalized world where all people are connected. He paid a special tribute to the past, to the people of Berlin, an 'isle of democracy' in the middle of former DDR. He reminded them of the famous words of another American president who'd visited Berlin many years ago, John F. Kennedy, and had uttered the words 'Ich bin ein Berliner' (I am a Berliner), standing on the western side of the Berlin Wall. He also reaffirmed that no wall can ever separate people from their desires for freedom, justice and peace. In 2017 and 2019 president Obama (now former president) came back to Berlin and spoke with the same charisma, to an equally enthusiastic crowd, in front of the Brandenburg Gate (2017) and at Rathaus (City Hall), to an audience of young leaders (2019). He spoke once more about the importance of tolerance and compassion among people, especially in the light of the new world reality.

Germany had experienced the large migrant wave of 2015 and 2016, with about a million people entering the country, mostly from war zones, and applying for asylum. It was heart breaking to see these images of desperate people, smuggled into Europe mostly by small insecure boats and then going by train or marching all the way to Germany, their 'promise land', risking their lives and all that they have earned in a life time, seeking for a better future. Due to the high standard of living in Germany, the country was the most desired destination among refugees. But this huge amount of people lacked, in many cases, any basic knowledge of German and also skills or qualifications that could help them quickly integrate into the German society and start earning a decent living. The religious factor (most of them were Muslims) also played a role in the reluctance expressed by parts of the German population, although the top political voice of Angela Merkel officially and publicly welcomed them. So their situation was critical. I had the opportunity, back in 2015, to visit a refugee shelter in the middle of Berlin. I was curious to see how they were treated and what their daily life looked like. What I saw was a lot of people, full of hopes but tired and bored, worried about their future, waiting sometimes for months for the processing of asylum and residency documents, living together in separate tiny spaces of a few square meters each, in a huge tent-like temporary construction. Children, women, men of all ages, united by the same dream of a better life on the German soil. I witnessed the lunch on a typical day in the camp: one boiled egg, a small piece of fried meat, a slice of bread and a small slice of cucumber on a paper plate, handed out by tireless volunteers. Nothing fancy but, for many, surely more than they could have had by staying in their native country, in war time. Seeing all these can certainly make you realize how much you have and, maybe, take for granted. I remember I came home that day and told everything not only to my husband but to my children also, so that they appreciate their smooth, worry-free life even more.

By 2016, more refugee shelters appeared in the city, one of them very close to our house, made up of white small containers perfectly aligned together, with alleys and flowers, like a small village in the middle of the city. Almost four years later, the 'village' is still in place…

During my stay in Berlin I had the chance to meet a lot of politicians and high-officials, who were also dealing with this migrant situation. They all spoke of the importance of tolerance and compassion among people but they also expressed the need to obey the laws of the country of adoption. Some migrants sadly showed little respect for the German values and often had problems with the Police. There have been some highly publicized cases of this kind and unfortunately, especially in the eastern part of Germany, it has brought a notable increase of the extremist parties in the polls, which seem to be on the rise in many countries in Europe, in recent years.

Due to my diplomatic status, I became a member of the 'Willkommen in Berlin' (WIB) club, the Diplomatic club, created and managed by the Ministry for Foreign Affairs in Berlin. This club has more than 400 members from more than 100 countries, all diplomats and diplomatic spouses. Its main purpose is to make the country known to its diplomatic members, to make the transition to the Berlin lifestyle easier and more pleasant and to provide a constant support and a meeting framework for its members. Once you register, you have access to more than 35 groups that you can join, depending on your interests. You can learn to draw, write Japanese, take professional photography lessons, play bridge, talk about English literature or learn to speak German. There is a bike club that organizes weekly escapes around Berlin, a theatre club that you can join and go with the other members to different shows, an architecture club, which takes you around the city to visit it and discover beautiful buildings and their history. I joined that one, the first year of my stay in Berlin. I really enjoyed our walks into town, meeting other diplomats and also famous architects. Each time someone was coming to show us hidden parts of Berlin, old buildings that maybe are less popular with tourists. This is how I found out about Hansaviertel in Berlin, the smallest district in the middle of the city, which was entirely destroyed during the WW II. Between 1957 and 1961 it was completely rebuilt, as a social housing project, with the large participation of some of the greatest architects at that time, from all Europe: Walter Gropius, Alvar Aalto, Ego Eiermann or Sep Ruf. It is now protected as a historical monument but you can walk through the alleys, visit its two churches or go by the apartment buildings, in their 60's style. We even had the chance to visit one apartment there. It was terribly small and the architect explained that the idea of the building was to house in young single people of the 60's. There were two separate parts of the building, each part with its own elevator and apartments for men, on one side and for women, on the other. Funny thing is that, as we saw the construction blueprints, we could easily figure out that the kitchens on the 'women's side' were a bit larger than on the 'men's side' of the building. I guess, although modern in conception and construction for those times, they still had these little stereotypes and misconceptions...

Another WIB group that I joined was 'History and Politics'. We were invited each month to discover parts of the country. Germany is a federal parliamentary republic consisting of sixteen partly-sovereign states (Bundesländer). Its capital, Berlin is considered a separate state on its own. It is the most populous country within European Union and one great economic power of the world. The states invited us regularly to visit their representation houses in Berlin (like normal embassies, one for each German state) and to discover traditional Germany and its beauty. They encouraged us to go visit places and also organized trips for the diplomatic community. Many places that I found out about during these meetings, we visited later with the whole family.

There were also diplomatic sport competitions that we gladly participated in, with good results, I might add☺. There was a diplomatic Tennis Tournament, a diplomatic Canoe Cup or a diplomatic Table-tennis Cup. They all helped unite the diplomatic corps, which is sometimes divided, mainly due to political rivalry. I have seen it with my own eyes, as it is also applied to diplomatic spouses' relationships... Some representatives of rival countries would categorically refuse to sit at the same table at events. Depending on which country, greater alliance or even geographical region they belong to, people tend to stick most of the time to their 'own kind of people'... or so to say... European countries, Arab countries, African countries or former members of the Soviet Union countries... so I guess, one of the main purpose and achievement of all these social events is to establish a human connection beyond country interests and rivalries.

As part of our diplomatic life, we were warmly received for a small visit by the German Chancellor Angela Merkel, also at the presidential Palace Bellevue, at Bundestag (Parliament) and Bundesrat (Federal Council). We visited Rathaus (Berlin City Hall) and talked to the mayor of Berlin.

Another part of my Berliner diplomatic life consisted of invitations to embassies and diplomatic residences in the city. Members of the diplomatic club opened up their doors and invited us to be their guests at formal lunches and dinners, cultural events designed to make their countries known. Some of these official residences and embassy buildings are genuine architectural jewels, with unique history and symbols. The beautiful building of the Romanian embassy, for instance, used to be a big postal office. My husband saw a picture of the majestic building, taken just after WW II. It was surrounded mostly by ruins and Russian tanks. Another marvellous embassy that I had the privilege to visit is the Italian embassy. It is located in a Venetian style palace, with highly decorated interiors. When you enter you might think you are visiting one of Italy's many wonderful museums. The embassy of Switzerland is the only official building in the centre that was left untouched during the heavy bombings in the war, due to Switzerland's neutrality. Great military precision, I would say... It is situated just a few steps from the modern government building, highly contrasting to it. The American, British and French embassies are also steps away from the Brandenburg Gate, all big impressive buildings, very well guarded too. The Nordic embassies in Berlin have also become a trademark of the city, with their common assembly of buildings, 'The Felleshus', home to embassies of Denmark, Finland, Iceland, Norway and Sweden, as a symbol of their historical Nordic bond, shared values and close cooperation. The complex is open to the public for visits, concerts and exhibitions, and everybody who passes by notices the copper band that surrounds the whole group of the five different buildings, each designed by native architects and arranged according to the geographical location on the map.

As I stand now on my terrace and write these pages, I realize my life in Berlin has been quite active and full of interesting events, many more than in Vienna. Of course, this is partly due to the fact that the kids were in school already, a bit more independent and, consequently, I could get involved in other activities away from home more often than before. As part of the diplomatic club, I went to an Ikebana workshop by a famous floral artist (organized by the Japanese embassy), I saw traditional dances from Paraguay, was deeply impressed by the formal 'Tea ceremony', also at the Japanese embassy and their unique traditions for New Year's celebration, I found out more about Christmas traditions in the UK and their afternoon tea with biscuits, I learned to cook Chinese dumplings, Indonesian rice cookies and Ukrainian traditional cold soup ('Borscht')...

I took my turn and had some small diplomatic gatherings at our house, at lunch or dinner, too. I tried to follow most of the guide lines in setting up a formal table. Accordingly, when doing this, you should always use a fine table cloth, preferably white, linen napkins (never paper!) for each guest, flowers and candles in the middle. I loved making these arrangements, we bought our own set of special small flower bowls to use, we got sets of fine crystal glasses for each type of drink and nice elegant plates to match. In order to be original and also more cost effective, I made flower arrangements myself, I also sewed a set of linen napkins with our national flag colours and cooked traditional Romanian recipes sometimes. When you set a formal table, you should always keep some very simple rules in mind: depending on the menu, you should have two plates of different sizes in front of each chair (with a decorative charger plate, larger that both, underneath), napkin placed on the top of the salad plate (the smaller one), knives on the right, blades facing the plates, forks on the left, spoon and dessert fork in front of the plates. Glasses (red wine, white wine and water) should be placed on the right, above the knives, forming a triangle, and butter plate and knife above the forks, on the left.

I was once invited, together with a group of diplomatic spouses, for a formal breakfast and a presentation at the most famous and beautiful hotel in Berlin, the grand Adlon. Besides the impeccable, delicious food we were served and the splendour of this old hotel facing the Brandenburg Gate, full of history reminders and meaning at every corner, we were also initiated in the art of napkin folding. We practiced some different styles... remember the white swans or ducks, made up of bath towels at some hotels, which wait for you on the bed each day?... this was the same... complicated wrappings that, I confess, were all far too elaborate to remember after I left ☺ So, I am still using the classical simple folding style that is never outdated.

Traditionally, the most important diplomatic event for each diplomat is the National Day Reception, held by each embassy every year on their National Day. It is a select gathering, with hundreds of important guests, high level politicians, government and local officials, other diplomats and also countrymen. I enjoyed these occasions every year, planning everything in advance. It was great to meet people I knew, all in one place and spend a pleasant evening with them, every December 1st (Romania's National Day).

A big event was also the annual Diplomatic New Year Reception, held mostly at some elegant hotel in town, with hundreds of diplomats and spouses celebrating together another year in a foreign country. Fine wine, gourmet food, good music and great company were the key to the success of this 'highlight of the season' event.

I have to tell you that all these events come by personal written invitation and confirmation of attendance is, most of the times, specifically required.

There were also good bye parties, sometimes very emotional, as someone dear was leaving for another destination and we never knew whether we would cross our paths again in this life... These parties are usually organized for the diplomat going away by other closed colleagues, but they are also done for the spouses. Ladies getting together to honor one of us leaving to another country. I took part in quite a few and they were all lovely but extremely emotional, as I already mentioned. When you form a close bond to somebody it is difficult to let go. Every summer, when a diplomatic year ends and another one is about to begin, some of the people you called friends for the last few years will be leaving, and with each of them, a small piece of your heart. One of my dearest friends in Berlin, Sejla, a diplomatic spouse from Bosnia, just left few months ago, so I feel now even more the sadness of such moments. Fortunately, with the fall of every year, another group of diplomats take office in Berlin and it is again time to make new acquaintances and to enjoy the old ones, while they are still around.

Over the years I have made nice friendships with spouses of diplomats from other countries, smart and kind ladies from all over the world: Tone from Norway, Svitlana and Olga from Ukraine, Yuka from Japan, Linda from Singapore, Fatima from Paraguay, Paloma from Spain or Petia from Bulgaria. No matter the age or destinations, they all lived a similar life and understand best the beauty and challenges that come with it. Yes, diplomatic life offers you the chance to meet fine people that maybe you would not normally meet, some of them with the same feelings and questions that you have about life.

I may not have a great career in my original profession, one that I'd envisioned years ago, but I made, like many of my fellow diplomatic spouses, a conscious choice that I have to live with and do not regret. We chose to support our husbands and to keep our family safe and united. Maybe the word 'sacrifice' is too strong, but sometimes I really felt like I have sacrificed my early dreams, my independence, the level of esteem and recognition that society shows you most of the times when you are a professionally accomplished person. There have been many moments and still are, when I think I have reached a terminus point and maybe I can no longer continue like this, that I need more, that I can do much more. And I am so sure most of my fellow diplomatic spouses felt the same, at least once. We dedicate all our time and efforts to our loved ones but also to best representing our countries, setting our dreams and aspirations aside. We have no official diplomatic rank or title but we are 'part of the package', sometimes only with a purely decorative presence, other times with active and permanent involvement, but always with the best intentions at heart and the desire to honor the countries we come from. As I heard it said many times, one should not underestimate the women's diplomatic power.

By the time I am writing these thoughts, we are probably in the last year of our diplomatic mission in Germany. I don't know what future holds for us, where we are going to move next. What other great destination just waits to be revealed? ... Nobody knows... only God. Although uncertainty can be frustrating for sure, we have to learn to embrace it and enjoy the present, not worry too much about the distant future. After all, this is a good life philosophy and, in fact my own life's motto: *'Enjoy life today, tomorrow is never promised'.*

Oberbaum Bridge Berlin

Konzerthaus Berlin

Hotel Adlon-breakfast table setting

Christmas market in Gendarmenmarkt

Locomotion in Berlin ☺

Fireworks across Berlin on New Year's Eve

Bavarian well-wishers on New Year's Eve in Garmisch

Zugspitze- the top of Germany

Festival of Lights- Berlin

Promoting Romania

The beautiful Elbphilharmonie in Hamburg

Formal dinner table set up at our house

View from Bastei Bridge- near Dresden

Wansee sandy beach

Winter time in Berlin

Volunteering for UNICEF

CHAPTER 4-

GUIDING PRINCIPLES

I think these principles will help anybody having an expat experience or moving temporarily to another country. Whether a diplomatic spouse or not, the experiences can be similar, up to a point, when moving abroad, and so the inherent difficulties.

These short guidelines will hopefully make the transition softer, your life a bit easier and take some pressure off your shoulders.

They are things that I have done or, I realize now, I should have done from the very beginning of my diplomatic journey, in order to have a smoother transition and a better experience.

They could lead you to live a good fulfilling life, feeling like home anywhere you move in the world.

Guidelines

1. Establish a routine (or keep one from home).
2. Make the new house your comfortable HOME, as it were your permanent residence.
3. Stay open to new habits.
4. Stay humble, don't forget where you started from.
5. Be friendly. Keep old friendships but also make new friends.
6. Don't compare people and places.
7. Respect the new customs and people.
8. Get involved, don't stay aloof.
9. Find groups you belong to.
10. Learn the local language.
11. Live the present and don't worry too much about the future.
12. MAKE THE MOST OUT OF IT!

CHAPTER 5-

SOME TRADITIONAL CUISINE

There is an old Romanian saying: 'love goes through the stomach'.

We, as diplomats, travel and live in different parts of the world, we live an amazing experience, sometimes fall in love with the places and also with the taste of some savoury local foods and dishes that become our favourites. We than carry the memories with us and, when we sometimes look back, we remind ourselves of a place and also the specific tastes that go with it.

These are some of the simple recipes that I have learned to cook while in Austria and Germany. They were among our family's favourites but I also cooked them for some of our guests, occasionally. They are traditional Austrian and German recipes, with my added small personal touch, to my own taste.

At the end I also added one of my favourite Romanian deserts, made by my grandma when I was little, always bringing back sweet childhood memories.

'Asparagus with butter'

I first tasted this recipe at my good Austrian friend, Beatrix. She cooked it one time when we were invited over.

Take a package of <u>green </u>fresh asparagus.

Peel it gently and then cut it into small circular pieces (2 cm each).

Warm a frying pan and add butter generously. Let it melt and then add the sliced asparagus. Add water to cover the content and then some salt and pepper.

Let it boil for around 10-15 minutes at medium heat.

The asparagus is fully cooked when it gets soaked.

Before you take it from the oven, add just a small spoon of sugar, as it makes it more tender and sweet.

Mix it all together.

You can serve it warm, as a side dish at the main course.

'Kaiserschmarrn'

This is one of my kids' favourite sweets from Austria and Bavaria. This is the recipe for 2 portions (for my children).

Take 200 g wheat flour, 30 g sugar, a touch of salt, 4 egg yolks and around 300 ml milk (I use soy or rice milk) and mix them all together in a bowl.

Mix firmly the egg white from 4 eggs separately in another bowl, until it gets stiff.

Add it then to the dough and mix it all together gently.

Warm a frying pan and add butter. Let it melt and then add the dough.

Let it cook for about 10 minutes, on both sides. It needs to look like a thick pancake, slightly golden brown.

Take it away from the oven and slice it into small irregular pieces.

Put it on plates, add apple puree, some raisins and then sprinkle sugar powder on top.

It is served warm, as a main dish or a dessert.

'Potato salad'

It is one of the most popular German dishes.

You need about 4 or 5 big potatoes. Peel them and cut them into thin slices or cubes.

Put a pot on the stove and boil the potatoes, fully covered with water.

Cook them for about 20-30 minutes, until they get soft and they break easily with a spoon.

Let them cool off and drain the water from the pot.

Peel and finely chop an onion and add it to the potatoes.

Stir, in a small bowl, 3 spoons of vinegar,one spoon of oil and some water, a sprinkle of salt and a small spoon of sugar, into a marinade.

Then pour it over the potatoes and mix it all together, without crushing the potatoes.

You can also add some chives or sliced boiled eggs, too (this is very similar to a Romanian dish).

The potato salad should rest for about 1 - 2 hours before serving, to allow all ingredients to properly mix.

It can be served as an appetizer or side dish, at main course.

'Viennese Schnitzel'

It is a popular dish also in Romania and in other countries, with only small preparation differences.

You can use chicken, veal or pork meat. I usually use chicken breast file. (250 g), although the traditional Viennese recipe usually requires veal meat.

Cut the meat into very thin slices. Actually this is one of the secrets of the Viennese schnitzel, the meat is extremely thin.

Add salt and pepper on the meat.

On a large plate put breadcrumbs. Cover it completely. (some use half wheat flour, half breadcrumbs, but I prefere breadcrumbs only).

Mix 3 eggs in a bowl.

Drag each piece of meat first through the breadcrumbs, until it is fully covered, then through the egg bowl and then again through the breadcrumbs, until it is fully covered.

Put it to fry in a pre-heated frying pan, with plenty of oil, and cook it on both sides (3-4 minutes) until it gets golden brown.

Take it out on a paper napkin, to absorb the extra oil.

Serve it warm or cold, with a slice of lemon on top. When in restaurants, they also serve it with cranberry jam.

'Apple strudel'

This original Austrian dish is one of our family's favourite winter desserts and I cooked it also for many of our guests.

Start by making the dough (I confess though, that most of the times, in order to save time, I use the pastry dough from the supermarket).

Mix together melted butter, wheat flour, warm water and a sprinkle of salt, until you get a smooth dough.

Let the dough rest in a warm small pot, covered for few minutes.

Start rolling out the dough and stretch it into a thin sheet, adding some flour, so that it does not stick while stretching.

Once you are ready with the dough, prepare the filling.

Peel the apples, chop them into fine small pieces, add sugar, cinnamon, a bit of rum and raisins and mix them all up.

Then let it rest for 5 minutes, so that the apples soften a little and mix with all the other ingredients.

Spread the filling all over the dough sheet and then roll it until it is completely sealed.

Brush it over with a bit of scrambled egg white and put it into the pre-heated oven (180-200 grad Celsius).

Let it bake for about 45 minutes.

Take it out when cooked and let it cool.

Slice it into thick pieces (rolls) and serve it with hot vanilla sauce on top or just add some sugar powder on top.

'Biscuit Salami'

I decided to include also a Romanian recipe to this list. It is one of my favourite deserts that brings back sweet childhood memories.

Ingredients:

- 500g biscuits
- 200 ml milk
- 150g butter
- 100g sugar (or other sweetener)
- 2 spoons cocoa powder
- 1 spoon rum
- Dried cherries, cranberries or raisins (if you wish).

Crush the biscuits into small pieces (but not too much!).

Melt the butter, warm the milk and then mix all ingredients together.

Let it rest for about 10 minutes.

Roll the mixture on a backing paper, into a 'salami' shape.

Secure the ends of the roll.

Put it into the fridge for few hours.

Cut it into slices and serve it cold.

Bon Appetite!

CHAPTER 6-

LOOKING BACK AND FORWARD

Looking back now at the last ten years of my life, I strongly believe that embarking to this journey was a good decision!

Of course, putting your whole life in boxes can be challenging but this kind of existence certainly helps you evolve. You finally understand how strong you can really be. You grow and you break free from clichés, you go out of your comfort zone so many times and test your mental strength, sometimes to the limits.

I am not going to lie, the uncertainty, not knowing where you will be in a few years, is certainly difficult. It stretches your nerves and puts you sometimes to the edge of tolerability. It's always comforting for the human mind to have landmarks: in three months you do this, in a year that... But when the end of a diplomatic posting comes, you no longer have these landmarks and then it's very difficult and stressful. But there's an old saying: 'make plans if you want to make God laugh'...

In the end, it is all worth it! Life flies anyway, so the more you experience, live and learn, the better you will feel when looking back.

You will discover, sometimes with great surprise and satisfaction that your own limits and tolerance are much higher that you have imagined before. You also learn to make a difference between old habits and real needs. This is of most importance and it will help you in life, in general!

When you move to another country you also realize how little someone really needs in life. Every time we moved away from Romania to another diplomatic posting, we took only about half of our possessions with us and then realized it was more than enough. Another diplomatic spouse told me once that the more you move, the less you will carry with you...

Of course, you will miss your family terribly, the loved ones that you are leaving behind and see only from time to time. Technology nowadays helps a lot and, over the years, has eased part of the homesick. I remember that, while I was an exchange high-school student in USA, years ago, I was writing letters to my parents and friends almost every day and I was hoping for letters from them in the mail box also daily... internet was then at the beginning and not everybody had access to it. Oh, how happy I was when I also got a photo into my letters!...Those days seem an eternity away and most of today's kids cannot even imagine living without WhatsApp, YouTube or other internet tools that they now simply use every day. Being able to communicate freely, at any time and with very low costs, can surely help when you are away. It makes you feel closer to the ones back home, you still feel present in their lives and don't have the impression that you miss much on things. But the reality is that you live different lives, your parents grow old without you by their side, your friends have good days and bad days that you don't get to share, everybody is moving on. You move on...

The most important, when living this life, is your partner. My husband and I are completely different. I am hot tempered, very organized and realistic (maybe too realistic), not too much into sports (I hate running... I am like 'if you ever see me running, run too, cause something bad is coming for sure ☺) while he is the definition of calmness, balance, always a dreamer, sometimes chaotic, forgetting where he put things or what was on his 'to do' list... But I think this is in fact one of our marriage's secrets... when I am angry he is calm, when I am worried about the future he paints it all bright, when he is superficial I double check, when he forgets things I am his 'walking agenda' and organizer. We went alone through happy but also difficult times and we managed to give each other support and strength.

When you live abroad you will also miss sometimes your favourite food, which not always can be found where you are. I remember sometimes craving for the simplest things, like a pretzel for example, that I could only find back in Romania. My husband always said he missed the sparkling water from back home, which tasted like no other, in his opinion.

But if you want to have a good life, you need to learn how to let go easily to places, things and people, how to gladly accept the challenges and wait for new adventures in your life. You have to embrace the novelty and transform it into your new habit, as it is the reality of that moment. After all, home is where you are together with your family... Bucharest, Vienna, Berlin or whatever... if we are together, it will always be our place.

I was always amazed at the ease with which our children adapted to each new destination. Although still very young, they have found the maturity and wisdom to overcome the burden inherent in any beginning. They have already changed three schools and have always taken it from scratch, like us, the parents. They made new friends, made themselves noticed by teachers and praised for their intellectual and human qualities. I bow in front of them! I can only hope that the future years will be as smooth as the ones before and that all this life experience will shape their character into becoming the fine adults that we, the parents, dream them to be. I hope they will be happy sharing this kind of life with us and, looking back, will think that it helped widen their horizon and refine their prospective. Usually kids of diplomats have no real deep roots. Mine were raised to be free, fully conscious of their origins but not too tied up, as international citizens, not too religious, not too attached to places and customs, that they might need to change or leave one day behind. A very wise woman told me once in Vienna that children are like arrows that parents need to point in the right direction and then, let go... So, I just pray we will choose the right direction for them...

I don't know where we will be in five years from now, in which country, on which continent. I have no idea how my life is going to be, but, after all, nobody really knows what future holds. Life is always unpredictable to all of us, whether we do realize it or not. I hope I will keep my inner peace and balance, my sense of purpose and I will find new ways to express myself and to devote my time to causes I believe in. I also hope that, in my senior years, I will look back with satisfaction and I will think: 'oh, what a fine ride my life was!'

When living the diplomatic life, time seems to stretch. You live in a few years as others in a life time, you see so many places and you end up with so many memories that keep adding and adding... You will always have these memories, but don't let them run your life. Let the past be gone and look forward to the future.

I realized that it usually takes around six months to start feeling at home in a new place, city or country. You gradually start developing new habits. You discover your new favourite restaurant at the corner of your street, your new preferred supermarket in the neighbourhood ... You even start having favourite songs in languages you didn't even like or understand some years ago. You make new friends, build up connections, you develop new habits, an entire new life routine.

Life becomes more and more settled and comfortable and then... it is time to move again...

ABOUT THE AUTHOR

ALEXANDRA PAUCESCU

Born and raised in Bucharest, Romania, she studied management and has a Master degree in business. She speaks five languages.

By the age of 30, she saw her whole life changing completely, as she married a diplomat and embarked on a life long journey as a trailing diplomatic spouse.

Inspired by this life twist, she decided to write a book, sharing the experiences and lessons learned throughout the years.

STAY IN TOUCH...

Follow 'Just a diplomatic spouse' on Facebook.

Facebook.com/justadiplomaticspouse

Follow Alexandra Paucescu on **Instagram**.

Please send your feedback and reviews on **Amazon**.

Thank you for reading this book!

Made in the USA
Middletown, DE
30 June 2020

11355331R00111